"God doesn't make mistakes. H
be the mother of your child. You
by developing your own personal MomSense—and this book
shows you how."

"Jean Blackmer offers moms a rare treat: a book that encourages women to trust their instincts and to think critically (to be skeptics, even!). Through fun-to-read, power-packing stories mixed with solid advice, Jean at once affirms, empowers, and equips moms to be the kind of moms God created them to be."

"Ever felt like somehow you missed mommy orientation class? Does it seem that all of the women in your play group got the secret kid manual and you were not on the distribution list? Take heart! In this amazing little book, you will discover all the gifts you already possess to be a great parent. After a dose of *MomSense* you can't help but be encouraged to be the kind of mom God designed you to be."

"You don't have to be perfect to be the perfect mom for your child. But you need an endless supply of *MomSense*. Here it is!"

"*MomSense* is a must-read for any mom who has ever wondered if she has what it takes to thrive during motherhood. As a mother of three preschoolers Jean reminded me, with wisdom gleaned from her own journey, that I can do this! She encouraged me, inspired me, and provided me with the resources to take action. Any mom who wants her parenting to make a difference should grab a copy."

Tracey Bianchi, pastor for women, Christ Church of Oak Brook; author, *Green Mama: The Guilt-Free Guide to Helping You and Your Kids Save the Planet*

"Do yourself a favor and bathe in the wisdom of this book—you'll emerge with more confidence and strength in what every mom has inside: the power to be a great mother."

Lisa T. Bergren, author, *Life on Planet Mom* and *The Busy Mom's Devotional*

"Reading *MomSense* is like spending time with a wise, warm friend, full of both challenge and grace."

Shauna Niequist, author, *Cold Tangerines* and *Bittersweet*

MomSense

A Common-Sense Guide to Confident Mothering

Jean Blackmer

Revell

a division of Baker Publishing Group
Grand Rapids, Michigan

© 2011 by Jean Blackmer

Published by Revell
a division of Baker Publishing Group
P.O. Box 6287, Grand Rapids, MI 49516-6287
www.revellbooks.com

Printed in the United States of America

Library of Congress Cataloging-in-Publication Data
Blackmer, Jean, 1964–
    Momsense : a common-sense guide to confident mothering / Jean Blackmer.
       p.   cm.
    Includes bibliographical references.
    ISBN 978-0-8007-2022-3 (pbk.)
    1. Motherhood—Religious aspects—Christianity. 2. Parenting—Religious aspects—Christianity. 3. Child rearing—Religious aspects—Christianity. 4. Mothers—Religious life. I. Title. II. Title: Commonsense guide to confident mothering.
    BV4529.18.B53 2011
    248.8′431—dc22   2010053531

Published in association with the literary agency of Alive Communications, Inc., 7680 Goddard Street, Suite 200, Colorado Springs, CO 80920, www.alivecommunications .com.

11   12   13   14   15   16   17   9   8   7   6   5   4   3

To every mom:
May you be confident
that God has created you
to be the mom your children need.

Contents

Foreword

Alright, let's just get this out of the way:

I've lost a child in Dillards.

I've pulled a flailing toddler out of the swimming pool, fully clothed.

I've put a child in time out and remembered him four hours later.

I've let my son eat cake for breakfast.

I've locked my kids in the backyard with a box of popsicles. A bunch of times.

Okay? So I live in the real world of motherhood. No intimidating "Mom of the Year" here. My successes have always cohabited with the failures, and the desire to be well thought of as a mom was quickly trumped by my desire to use motherhood as material. (If your life is a circus, become a writer and make a living off the chaos. You're welcome.)

So what am I adding to the three zany kids I already have? That's right. Two more from Ethiopia. The mom who once drove by herself from Austin to Wichita with three kids under five—who snapped somewhere during hour seven between the crying and pooping and screaming and pulled over on I-35, locked the kids in the car, and sat in the grass twenty feet away staring at her children mouthing "MOMMY!!!" with their faces pressed to the window while she sobbed for ten minutes—is adopting two more kids. On purpose.

"Why?" you must be asking.

Because basic MomSense overrides my fears and failures and reminds me that motherhood is my greatest adventure to date. Being a great mom doesn't mean being a perfect mom; that's not the deal we enter when we bring that first gangly baby home. Every mom fails, every mom feels overwhelmed, every mom cries, every mom blows it so profoundly she is not sure she can even tell her friends—and would certainly maim or kill to keep the story out of earshot of her mother-in-law.

But the other side of the story includes the moments when your children are piled on your lap as you read to them in funny voices while they snuggle into the crook of your arm. It certainly includes your attempts to keep a straight face when your daughter says the funniest thing that has ever been said, while you pretend to take her seriously and then rush to call your mom. It is that spot on the back of your son's neck after a bath that dares you not to kiss the tarnation out of it. It's the tender moments when you wipe tears and kiss dirty faces and hold little hands and brush out hair. It is a love so encompassing and overwhelming you feel like you could perish under the weight of it.

It's our MomSense, the same instincts that wrap our children in security and affirm their worth in this big world. I have it. You have it. It is the language of motherhood. Let us continue to create a community of mamas who hold our failures loosely and embrace laughter, love, and the adventure of parenting with gratitude for the responsibility and grace for the journey. This ride is brief; let's not miss a second of it.

With much love,
Jen Hatmaker, author of *Out of the Spin Cycle*

Acknowledgments

Writing a book is a team effort, and I have had the privilege of working with an amazing group of people.

A BIG thanks to:

Brittany Berger, Michelle Holmberg, Nikki Kennedy, Jacque Moore, and Shannon Wange: thanks for your honest input, stories, advice—and most of all, for sharing your lives with me.

Naomi Cramer Overton, Shelly Radic, and Carla Foote: thanks for your wise leadership and faithful encouragement.

Elisa Morgan, Carol Kuykendall, Mary Beth Lagerborg, Karen Parks, and Tom Webb: thanks for initiating the concept of MomSense and helping moms make sense out of mothering.

The staff at MOPS International: thanks for all you do, especially for the contributions you've made toward this book. As a ministry to moms we've seen this concept of MomSense grow, beginning with the *MomSense* radio program that had a good run for fifteen years, the ongoing encouragement to moms in the *MomSense* magazine, and now this book. I'm excited to see how this impacts the lives of the moms we long to help.

Andrea Doering, Twila Bennett, Michele Misiak, and the whole team at Revell: thanks for the amazing talents you bring to make this book come alive and encourage moms everywhere.

Lee Hough and Andrea Heinecke with Alive Communications: thanks for believing in this book idea and working to make it a reality.

Josh, Jordan, and Jake Blackmer: endless thanks to you for providing lots of good writing material, and for bringing so much joy and adventure into my life.

Zane: without you I would be lost—not just because I have a horrible sense of direction, but also because I need you as my faithful friend and partner. Love you forever.

Introduction

Mom Intuition + Common Sense = MomSense

Mom intuition is something a woman brings to mothering, something that is often not really learned, just known—a hunch, an inkling, a sixth sense, or a gut feeling.

Common sense is using good sense and sound judgment in practical matters. Sometimes common sense incorporates a mom's intuition, but it is also something she can learn and improve upon to establish her mothering skills.

Mash together a mom's intuition and common sense and you have MomSense.

A woman develops her reliance on the combination of her intuition and common sense as she grows into her role as a mother—as she becomes the confident, reliable, secure, loving mom her children need.

When I first became a mom, on a MomSense scale from one to ten—with ten being excellent and one being completely clueless—I was about a two and a half. Okay, maybe a little closer to a three.

clueless 1   • ▲ •   •   •   •   •   •   •   10 excellent

I had absolutely no "mommy training." Like many of us, I had more training in learning to drive a car than I had in learning the skills of raising another human being.

I hardly ever babysat. I hardly ever thought about being a mom. I was pretty focused on my education and career. Then I fell in love. We got married, and after a few years decided we would like to have a baby. We made the decision to get pregnant like one makes the decision to eat a turkey sandwich. We didn't spend much time thinking about this decision or analyzing what it would mean and how it would change our lives—we just did it and didn't look back.

Months later, looking at this little guy in my arms in the hospital, I felt a love like never before. I also felt a sense of purpose and responsibility like never before—and I felt completely terrified. I knew I was in way over my head. I suddenly needed a crash course in taking care of an infant. I watched most of the movies at the hospital, questioned the nurses incessantly, and then bravely set out from the hospital to bring this little thing home and take care of him with Zane, my husband and my partner in clueless parenting.

For example, I don't remember anyone telling me about the sticky black poo. Zane had done all of the diaper changing at the hospital. So, when I changed my first diaper ever in my life and saw this black gunk, I thought something was terribly wrong with my baby. I called the nurse in a panic. She calmly told me this was normal.

Marisa De Los Santos, author of the novel *Love Walked In*, says it eloquently when she writes about parenthood.

No matter what the circumstances, parenthood is thrust upon a parent. No one is ever quite ready; everyone is always caught off guard. Parenthood chooses you. And you open your eyes, look at what you got, say "Oh my gosh," and recognize that of all the balls there ever were, this is the one you should not drop.[1]

When I became a mom, I felt overwhelmed with the responsibility of raising another human being. This was definitely not a ball I wanted to drop. So although I was clueless, I was (and still am) teachable. I read books, talked to other moms, joined a moms group, processed constantly with Zane, prayed more than I've ever prayed in my life, called our doctor often with questions, and pretty much learned through trial and error. Experience is a great tool for learning—both the successes and the failures.

I'll never live down one of my many blunders.

One morning my firstborn son, Josh, who was probably ten months old at the time, woke up starving. He was crying inconsolably. I placed him in his highchair, opened the fridge—and realized we were out of baby food. Desperate to get food into his mouth and get him to stop screeching, I spied a jar of all-natural, no sugar added jelly. *Hmm, that looks good. Same consistency as baby food and mostly fruit, right?*

I opened the jar of jelly, grabbed our little airplane-shaped baby spoon out of the kitchen drawer, and started feeding Josh spoonfuls of purple jelly. He loved it! Like a baby bird, he would open his mouth before I could refill the spoon, ready for his next bite. He clenched his hands with excitement and kicked his feet gleefully. Then Zane walked in.

"Um, honey, I don't think he should be eating that," he suggested.

"Why not? It's mostly fruit and the label says no sugar added. And look at him—he loves it," I said, as I spooned some more jelly into Josh's mouth. Then a strange gurgling sound came from him. Suddenly, purple goo covered the tray of his highchair. He spit it all up and, of course, started crying again. I felt awful. I honestly didn't know that would happen.

Today Josh still won't eat jelly, but he did survive and is thriving as a nineteen-year-old college student. In fact all three of our boys survived. As time went on I learned more and more about myself, my strengths, my weaknesses, when to trust my gut, and when to call in others for advice. I don't know what I would have done without my husband, Zane, a true partner in parenting, as well as my family and friends. I was especially grateful to form a close group of mom-friends who shared my struggles and my dilemmas, and who became my go-to girls for advice—a group of friends I'm honored to still be connected to.

Even though I didn't begin with a high score on the Mom-Sense scale, I absorbed information like a sponge and sought help from friends, family, and mentors, and then applied what I learned to my mothering. I am still in the process of learning, and like you, I want to be the best mom I can be.

In a recent study on motherhood, a rigorous, large scale investigation was conducted by a team of social science researchers from the University of Minnesota, the University of Connecticut, and the Institute for American Values. This study discovered that nearly 93 percent of mothers surveyed agreed that a mother's contribution to the care of her child is so unique that no one can replace it, and nearly 81 percent of mothers said mothering is the most important thing they do. These same women also assigned a very high priority to the desire to improve their parenting skills. In spite of all the other opportunities women have today, these mothers still believe being a mom is the most important thing they do, and they want to do it well.[2]

I hope we'll begin by combining what we know with what we learn, adding a willingness to grow, and then confidently trusting our own MomSense. That's what this book is all about: being confident in our roles as mothers, trusting our intuition, and developing the skills we need to confidently raise our little ones.

This book contains lots of mom stories, mom quotes called "MomSense from Other Mothers" taken from a survey of five hundred moms, expert opinions, and thought-provoking "Your MomSense" questions at the end of each chapter to do on your own or in a group. We've even included a whole chapter for practice in using your MomSense with "Mama Drama" scenarios.

My hope and prayer is we'll discover more about ourselves and the unique gifts we all bring into our mothering practices. I say "practices" on purpose, because mothering is a constant learning process. We never really learn it all, because things change from issue to issue, child to child, and woman to woman. This book is not meant to tell anyone what to do, but to help each individual mom decide what is best for herself and her family as she experiences this stage of life known as motherhood—a journey that changes us forever, constantly challenges us, and helps us grow into better, stronger, more confident mothers.

Here we go . . .

MomSense from Other Mothers

MomSense is...

The uncanny understanding moms have of the chaos that is their usual way of life. It means intimately knowing what is best for your child and interpreting the garbled request of a toddler. It is the sense moms make of what others would say is beyond human ability to grasp. —Lori, mom of three

A special sixth sense enabling us to be the best moms we can be to our child . . . the little voice that should be listened to when you don't know what to do. —Melissa, mom of one

As a mom, knowing what is best and what works for your child. We all have different viewpoints, but when you become a mom you become an expert on your child. —Laci, mom of three

That super-power that tingles when it's too quiet in the house and you know the kids are up to no good. —Becky, mom of three

That God-given ability that combines common sense, education, intuitiveness, and personal history to nurture our families. —Harriet, mom of six

A unique understanding of the daily challenges of being a mom. —Lisa, mom of two

Feelings moms have about situations that others may not understand. —Reyna, mom of one

It is all about being confident as a mother. You get a certain "sense" about you when you have children. —Nicole, mom of three

Section I

Discovering Your MomSense

Who doesn't love to open presents?

Excitement stirs within us as we gaze upon a delightfully wrapped package and anticipate what's inside. Then some of us carefully undo the tape, fold up the wrapping paper, and save it to use again—while others rip off the paper and toss it aside. But most of us can't wait to see what treasure this gift holds. It's something that someone selected specifically for us, knowing our personalities, our likes, and our needs.

Discovering our MomSense is a little like opening up an extraordinary box with a magnificent bow on top. This box holds a special gift inside designed especially for each and every mom.

It's time to open this gift and learn about your own distinctive MomSense. Unwrap and expose this mysterious combination of a mom's intuition and common sense that exists inside her.

So let's get started and unwrap the gift that's been waiting to be revealed in each of us—our unique MomSense.

1

Growing Your Common Sense

Common sense is instinct. Enough of it is genius.

George Bernard Shaw

The most familiar definition of common sense is "good sense and sound judgment in practical matters." However, it's really not an easy concept to nail down. The first time I really started to think about common sense was in a bizarre setting not too long ago, when I was part of a group being considered to sit on a jury for a murder trial.

You know the feeling when you get a jury summons: you think, *Please no, I hope I don't have to actually serve!* and you want to fling it in the trash, but you know you can't. You just have to do it. When I received mine, it turned out to be for an awfully gloomy case about a man charged with first-degree murder.

Knowing the seriousness of the case, the feeling that I was doing something important started to emerge. I sensed I was doing something really valuable for society. Questions swirled through my mind. *What if this man is innocent? What if he was defending himself? What if it was a cold-blooded, planned murder? What is the truth here?* I found myself completely engaged.

Then the elimination process of jurors began. Each juror was asked questions by the judge, and many were excused from duty. When one person was allowed to leave, the judge would call a name to replace that person. After about an hour of this elimination, my name was called and I was asked to step into the jury box. I was nervous as the judge methodically asked me all the previous questions to get me up to speed with the other potential jurors. Then when she finished questioning us, it became the lawyers' turn.

The defense attorney immediately brought up the whole issue of reasonable doubt and common sense. The man was guilty of murder, but it was not so clear-cut on whether it was murder in the first or second degree, and a fine line existed between the definitions of those charges. Therefore, he emphasized that the prosecution must prove to the satisfaction of the jury beyond a reasonable doubt the existence of all the elements necessary to constitute the crime charged. Then he put up a slide on the wall that read:

> Reasonable doubt means a doubt based upon reason and *common sense* which arises from a fair and rational consideration of all of the evidence, or lack of evidence, in the case.

If you watch any crime television dramas then you know most lawyers emphasize the idea of reasonable doubt, but this lawyer emphasized common sense. He started questioning us along this line of reasoning, starting with me.

"Ms. Blackmer. I see here that you are a mom. Is that correct?"

"Yes, I have three boys," I responded.

"Would you say in your role as a mother you have to use your common sense often?"

"Absolutely, every day," I answered.

"How would you define common sense?"

This caught me by surprise, so I stumbled around a bit. "Um, well, I guess common sense is something you just know to be true and most other people would agree with you. It's sort of basic knowledge of what's right and what's wrong." I began to realize how hard it is to nail down this idea of common sense.

"How would you apply your common sense to this case?" he asked.

"Well . . . I guess I would have to hear and see all the evidence, listen to the testimonies of the witnesses, listen to the expert opinions such as how the man died, listen to my fellow jurors and then make the best decision I could with what I hear and what I know, and what my gut tells me."

As the process continued, his questions really caused me to think about what I believe and why. It was fascinating to hear how others in the group answered. No one seemed to be right or wrong. We all had very different answers, yet they were all logical and valid responses. I also noted how everyone respected each other's opinions whether they agreed or disagreed. It was like we were all open to what everyone else had to say and were learning from each other.

I couldn't help but see the parallel between my life and what I was experiencing in this solemn little courtroom. We were going to be called upon to use our common sense and come to a decision regarding the future of another human being. As moms, we use our MomSense every day to shape the future of those in our sphere of influence—our children, our husbands, our friends—and to impact who these people will become. We speak into their lives in a magnificent way. And a big part of our MomSense is our common sense.

In mothering, common sense—using good sense and sound judgment in everyday, practical matters—is a huge factor in how a mom decides what she decides, why she chooses to live the way she does, and even how she responds to different situations. We seek information and listen to other opinions, yet we all come to different conclusions. Every mother is as unique as her own fingerprint.

This courtroom experience was enlightening. It was an amazing exercise in self-discovery. I had to think about what I believed, and express my beliefs and reasoning to a bunch of strangers. When I left the courtroom, I had grown personally through the whole process. And even more strangely, I felt I knew the other people with whom I had spent the past day and a half. We had this bond due to the time we had spent together. Not only did I know what they each did for a living and if they had ever read murder mysteries, I also knew what they believed on very sensitive issues. We had listened to each other and had respected our differences. It was fascinating.

I wanted to take what I had learned and pass it on to mothers because I think learning about our common sense and articulating our beliefs are great opportunities for personal growth and will enhance our mothering skills. Even the process of defining common sense is a good exercise.

MomSense from Other Mothers

What is common sense?

Common sense is something most of us have. It's something that tells us not to eat the yellow snow or not to cross the road if a car is coming. —Kimberly, mom of three

An understanding of common life issues like right from wrong. Example: not picking your nose in public. —Stefani, mom of two

The "well, duh" kinds of things. —Heather, mom of two

Common sense is what makes sense to everyone . . . except the kids. —Becky, mom of three

Are we all created with an equal amount of common sense? Don't we all know somebody who is really smart but does not possess much common sense? I know several people like that. They're brilliant scientists, math professors, doctors, or English teachers, but when it comes to just plain street smarts, they come up short. Here's an example. When I was in high school, my friend and I decided to bake some cookies. The recipe said to "grease the bottom of the pan," so she did exactly that: she began to spread butter on the underside of the cookie sheet. I remember thinking, *How in the world does she not know what that means?*

So, no, I don't believe we all possess the same level of common sense, but I do believe as we experience life we can learn common sense. The Bible even encourages us to live sensibly, especially the book of Proverbs, which is filled with practical living advice. Proverbs 16:22 says, "Good sense is a fountain of life to him who has it, but the instruction of fools is folly" (ESV).

Let's challenge ourselves to really think about how we use our common sense, and how this enhances our MomSense.

Your MomSense

- Do you think you have a high level of common sense? Why or why not?
- What experiences have you had that developed your common sense?
- How do you use your common sense in your mothering practice?
- How can you help your children develop their common sense?
- Take a minute to write down your own definition of common sense:

_____

_____

_____

2

Mom and You

In search of my mother's garden, I found my own.

Alice Walker

There is absolutely no doubt about it: one of the greatest events in my life so far has been becoming a mother. The gift of caring for and loving another human being who, at first, was totally dependent on me awakened a new "me" that I didn't know existed. The lifelong journey of learning to put others' needs ahead of my own was amplified when I became Mom. Motherhood has challenged me to live beyond myself in a whole new way. And because of the profound love between a mom and each of her children, and the connection between two people that such a bond creates, a desire to give all of myself for the sake of someone else was ignited.

Basically, motherhood made me grow up.

Growing up, making the shift from childhood to adulthood, can be both exciting and painful at times. The same is true of growing up in motherhood. The new experiences and feelings of motherhood, such as watching a baby grow before your very eyes, are among the greatest wonders of the world. At the same time, motherhood is exhausting and can challenge you like nothing you have experienced before.

Part of growing up is getting to know ourselves, learning about our gifts and our weaknesses, and understanding who we are and how we became that person. This, for most women, brings us back to our own mothers.

The mother/child relationship will shape all your other relationships. In *The Mom Factor: Dealing with the Mother You Had, Didn't Have, or Still Contend With*, Henry Cloud and John Townsend emphasize:

> Not only does the quality of your relationship with your mother dictate how things go between the two of you, it also drastically impacts all areas of your life. Not only do we learn our patterns of intimacy, relating, and separateness from mother, but we also learn about how to handle failure, troublesome emotions, expectations and ideals, grief and loss, and many of the other components that make up our "emotional IQ"—that part that guarantees whether or not we will be successful at love and work. In short the following two realities largely determine our emotional development:
> 1. How we were mothered.
> 2. How we have responded to that mothering.[1]

Being a mom is a huge responsibility, but that's part of growing up too. When we accept this responsibility and do the best we can—not to achieve perfection, but to learn from our past and apply it to our present—we can look forward to our future.

Learning from Your Past

For most of us, our experiences with our mothers were a blend of both good and bad. Our mothers were not perfect; they did some things right and some things wrong. So many times we begin to "mother bash," and that's not the point here. The point is to discover and grow in your MomSense, using your past experiences to become the best mom you can be.

MomSense from Other Mothers

What moms said about how their own moms influenced their mothering:

I learned that motherhood involves a great deal of unnoticed work. I also learned things I don't want to repeat. —Sara, mom of three

We didn't hear the words "I love you" very much growing up, although we all felt loved. I tell my kids I love them about fifteen times a day. —Cindy, mom of three

I know how to have fun with my kids. She taught me to jump in the rain puddles with them. —Michelle, mom of three

I usually define myself in opposition to my mother. I didn't like how she mothered me. —Gabriele, mom of one

I am really laid back. My mom was a hippie so I am kind of relaxed too. —Heather, mom of four

She taught me to trust my instincts. —Annalise, mom of one

My mom is incredible! I try to be as calm as she is and love my babies as much as she loved me and my sister. She influences how I mother every day. —Christine, mom of two

For some of you who do not have a close relationship with your mom or do not have positive mom experiences, this process of thinking about your past might be painful. If this is true for you, please talk to someone you can trust: a counselor, pastor, friend, or mentor who can help you through this process. Maybe you have someone else in your life whom you admire, such as a grandmother or an older sister. Think about the positive impact she has on your life and your mothering.

Let's take a moment to answer the following questions and think about the gifts our moms have given us:

1. What do you love most about your mom?
2. What are your mom's strengths?
3. What are you most proud of about your mom?
4. What has your mom had to overcome?
5. What are some values your mom instilled in you?
6. What is your favorite memory of your mom?
7. How did your mom express her love to you?

Next, let's spend some time thinking about how we would like to be different than our moms.

Expert Opinion

If you were not emotionally close to your mother, it may be difficult for you to bond with your own child. Here are some tips on how to grow in your ability to bond emotionally with others, adapted from *Secrets of Your Family Tree: Healing for Adult Children of Dysfunctional Families*.

- Find a safe, uncritical relationship or two in which you can begin to learn to bond. Bonding wilts in the face of detachment or criticism, but flowers in the presence of acceptance and warmth.
- Be aware of your resistance to intimacy. Do you withdraw when you find yourself becoming needy? Do you devalue relationships when you are hurt?
- Take risks with emotional issues. Is there something you have never told anyone? If so, risk telling this to a person you've found as your safe, uncritical person, and allow them to help you with this burden.
- Challenge yourself to share your emotions at a deep level with others.
- Allow yourself to feel the need for closeness. God created us to need others, and you'll find this type of closeness with other human beings fills your soul.
- Pray on a personal level rather than with a "grocery style" list of needs.
- Meditate on who God is rather than what he does.
- Begin to forgive those who have hurt you. (You may need help to do this from a trusted friend, pastor, or counselor.) Remember: "hurt people, hurt people," so whoever hurt you was probably hurt by someone too.
- Allow for mistakes. Practicing bonding means sometimes getting hurt in the process. You'll learn who is safe and who isn't. With practice you will learn the skill and personal rewards of emotional closeness with others.[2]

1. What is it about your mom that you struggle with the most?
2. What are some of your mom's weaknesses?
3. What do you wish you and your mom could do together?
4. What would you like to do differently than your mom did?

Have you heard the story about the young mom who was cooking a roast for her family, and her five-year-old daughter noticed how she cut off the rump before putting it in the pan?

"Mom, why do you do that?" she asked.

"Hmmm, I don't really know, it's just how my mom did it." Later that day, the young mom asked her mom why she always cut off the back end of the roast.

"That's just how my mom always did it," she replied. "Let's ask Grandma."

They went into the living room and asked Grandma why she always cut off the rump of the roast before cooking it.

"It didn't fit in my roasting pan," she stated.

Seriously, we bring some of our actions and behaviors into our mothering simply because it's what our moms did. Without any thought of self-evaluation, we just do it because it's what we know—like cutting off the rump of a roast for no good reason. Some of those actions, behaviors, and beliefs are positive qualities to pass on from generation to generation—and some need to be left behind. So let's take some time to do a little self-discovery about why we do what we do, or why we believe what we believe, and grow in our journey to develop our MomSense and become the moms we want to be.

Writing Your Story

Moms, let's remind ourselves frequently that "love covers a multitude of sins" because no one does everything right. As much as motherhood has awakened a stronger and more loving spirit in me, it has also opened my eyes to areas in which I am weak. We all bring some of our history into our current situation. Some of us have really tough stories and lots of challenges to overcome, but with the help of God and others, we can rewrite our scripts if needed.

In Donald Miller's book *A Million Miles in a Thousand Years*, he tells of his opportunity to rewrite the story of his life. He was asked to make a movie about a memoir he wrote, but when he met with the two film producers they said he needed to make his life a little more exciting for it to be a successful movie. In the process of re-creating the fictional Don for the movie, he realized he might write great stories, but he wasn't living a great story.

> I was creating the person I wanted to be, the person worth telling stories about. It never occurred to me that I could re-create my own story, my real life story, but in an evolution I had moved toward a better me. I was creating someone I could live through, the person I would be if I redrew the world, the character that was me but flesh and soul other. And flesh and soul better too.[3]

He goes on to tell how he began to live a better story. He found his absent father, stopped watching TV, biked across America, started a non-profit, and fell in love. He began living a story, not just imagining it—and he filled his life with risk, possibility, beauty, and meaning.

When we become mothers, we have the opportunity to write our future story. We can make changes in our lives that will profoundly affect both our future and the future stories of our children. We can improve on the positive aspects of our experiences and learn from the experiences we want to change. We do not have to repeat the mistakes of our moms; instead, we can learn from them and become the moms we want to be.

Mom Story

Finding Me

    My mom was a serious perfectionist. She had OCD (obsessive compulsive disorder). We had to keep a perfectly clean house; I mean the house had to be spotless. Not a speck of dust. One of my chores was to take a Q-tip and clean all the light switches. She couldn't stand it if the light switches had any grime or fingerprints on them. I just thought this was normal, because it was all I knew.

When I married, became a mom, and had a home of my own, I was always "shoulding" myself. *I should keep my house cleaner. I should put all the dishes away. I should get the laundry done. I should dust off the bookshelf. I should do this or I should do that*, I would tell myself—until I finally realized I shouldn't. It was okay if I didn't. It was free-ing to reach that decision, especially because I can give my kids a different experience than what I had as a little girl.

When my second baby was born, my mom came to help. My husband and I were nervous because we weren't sure how her OCD would affect her when she experienced our home. But my mom surprised me. When she showed up, one of the first things she said was, "If I'm doing something that's not helpful, let me know. I want to support you and how you want to parent your kids." And she's done that.

I think I'm still figuring out how to be who I want to be, separate from my mother. I recently pierced my nose, partly because I knew my mom wouldn't approve and partly because it was a state-ment declaring myself as an individual. I'm growing into the "me" I want to be and becoming more confi-dent as I figure myself out.

Chelsea, mom of two

Don't we all feel like that at times, still trying to separate ourselves from our mothers and still conflicted about gaining their approval? Whether our mothers were "normal" or "abnormal" (someone once said "normal" is just a setting on the dryer), we are all trying to become our unique selves. And most likely our mother is still learning how to let us live a separate life from her own—like Chelsea's mother, who recently admitted she screwed up a lot as a mom and wanted Chelsea to know she was willing to do things differently as a grandma. What an awesome thing for a mom to say—to admit her mistakes, to be willing to change, and to respect Chelsea's and her husband's choices on how to parent.

And now Chelsea is rewriting her script. She's choosing to live a different story than the one she began with. She's beginning a new story in the lives of her children and using her past experiences for good, for both her and her children's future.

No one has influenced who we are today more than our mothers, and we will have a similar incredible influence on who our children will become. Knowing who we are and what strengths and weaknesses we bring into our mothering practices enhances our ability to do this mothering thing well. (Not perfect. Remember, that's not the goal.)

We have the opportunity to be a character in a great story and transform into the women we want to be. We can be a good example to our children of not repeating the same mistakes we or our own mothers have made, and we can confidently lead our children into an exciting life filled with purpose and meaning.

We are the beginning of many stories, and looking positively toward our future will help create an atmosphere in our homes of hope, adventure, and excitement as we continue this journey of mothering.

Your MomSense

- List three strengths you can apply to your mothering from your relationship with your mom:

  _____

  _____

  _____

- Now list three weaknesses you have developed due to your mom's influence that you can improve upon in your own life:

  _____

  _____

  _____

- What biases or blind spots did you discover you might have in your own mothering practice as you thought about your mom's influence?
- If your child were to describe you to a friend, what would you hope he or she would say?

3

What's a Mama to Do?

It's not hard to make decisions when
you know what your values are.

Roy Disney

Betsy and her husband, Ben, sat at their kitchen table looking
out the window of their apartment on the thirty-fifth floor
of a high-rise in Manhattan, while their six-month-old baby,
Polly, slept peacefully in her crib in her nursery. Below, cars
whizzed by and sirens blared. From their loft they could see
the Empire State Building, Times Square, and the Statue of
Liberty. The noise of the city ricocheted off the buildings;
they could even hear two men shouting at each other about
a parking spot.

Living in the city had been an incredible adventure. They had made great friends and enjoyed the past six years. Betsy was finishing up her PhD in social psychology and was teaching at a university. Ben was an engineer. They worked hard, juggling their schedules to be with Polly as much as they could. But this hectic lifestyle was taking its toll. Usually Ben didn't come home until around 7 p.m., when Polly was grumpy from the day and ready to go to bed. Betsy was weary of juggling her studies, her work, and her role as a mom. They had saved up some money and decided it was time to make a change.

For years they had dreamed of starting their own business, and they had decided they wanted to buy an apple orchard in Maine and start producing apple cider.

"Are we crazy?" Betsy asked Ben. "People can't understand why you would leave your job as an engineer and why I wouldn't pursue a career using my PhD."

"We're not crazy," Ben said, as he reached out and held her hand. "If this doesn't work out we can always fall back on jobs we've been trained for."

"I know. I can't believe we're doing this, though. I'm a little scared."

"Me too," Ben said.

Ben, Betsy, and Polly said goodbye to their New York friends and left that life behind. They started a new life adventure on six acres of land with two hundred apple trees. They purchased a '50s style ranch home and took turns each day working the orchard and taking care of Polly. They bought trees, battled beavers that snuck onto their land, and started producing and selling their first batch of apple cider.

Betsy and Ben based their decision to make a change in their lives on their values, such as spending time together as a family, being outdoors, and supporting local businesses. They don't know yet if it is all going to work out, but Betsy told me, "Just the other day we were all outside walking through our orchard. Polly was carrying a little basket and filling it with dandelions. I looked at Ben and smiled, because I really love this life."

Time will tell if this venture will be successful or not, but they don't regret the decision they made.

Life is jam-packed with decisions. How does a person make decisions and live without regret like Ben and Betsy?

All the decisions a woman has to make in a single day, let alone in a lifetime, can be overwhelming. As moms, decision making is multiplied exponentially because we are not only making decisions for ourselves but also for our children, especially when they are still young. I started to count my decisions for one day, but by 9 a.m. I was already at decision number 473. At this point I figured counting my daily decisions was practically impossible and certainly a waste of my time. So, I didn't. But I do know as women and moms we make gobs of decisions—and then many of us fret about them and wonder if we've made a mistake.

Most of our daily decisions may seem small and insignificant, while other decisions may be very important. In a typical day, moms may have to decide what to eat, what to make our children for breakfast, lunch, dinner, and snack time, which socks to put on, and what products to buy at the grocery store. Added to these are the more weighty decisions such as whether or not to call the doctor again for a sick baby, if we should go back to work—and if so, who in the world will be our daycare provider and how much will it cost—or what school to select for our child. All of these decisions and thousands of others, big and small, are related to our mom role. On top of all that, we often have to make decisions that may exist outside of our mom world. And it's not just the number of choices we need to make each day;

what really ramps up the stress is the abundance of options we face with each choice.

I experienced this overwhelming choice scenario recently when we remodeled our house. My husband works in real estate development, and we bought a fixer-upper and lived in it for seven years. Then we decided to redo it with the hopes of eventually selling it. The number of decisions we had to make during the remodel was ridiculous. But they still had to be made. We spent countless hours looking at doorknobs, sinks, faucets, tile, and paint colors. At times I was so overwhelmed I just caved; I didn't care anymore. I couldn't make another decision. Sometimes I begged my husband or the salesperson to "please just choose for me." I love what comedian Erma Bombeck had to say about this: "I have a theory about the human mind. A brain is a lot like a computer. It will only take so many facts, and then it will go on overload and blow up." Ever feel like that? I know I have.

As I researched decision making for this book, I discovered this concept of "choice overload" is not unique to me. In fact, it's quite common. I thought having such an abundance of choices would be a good thing, but it turns out it can cause extreme anxiety and dissatisfaction.

A mom recently described her experience of this to me. When she was trying to decide how to get her little girl to fall asleep in her crib, she started asking around and searching the Internet for ideas on what to do. Some people said to let her daughter cry herself to sleep; some said to never let her cry herself to sleep. She also found just about every other option in between. "I was so overwhelmed with all the different opinions," she explained.

> I was totally confused and had no idea what to do. My husband and I went back and forth about which options to try. Not having any clear direction, we just muddled our way

through it with our little girl. But she just kept crying when we put her in her crib. Finally, we were so drained we decided to let her cry it out. That worked for us, and now she sleeps just fine. But it was such a hard process for me to make up my mind because of all the information and all the different options.

In *The Paradox of Choice: Why More Is Less*, author Barry Schwartz describes a study where college students were asked to evaluate a variety of gourmet chocolates. Some students were asked to compare six varieties of chocolates and others compared thirty varieties. (I'd like to have participated in this study.) The students were then asked to choose which chocolates they would select for themselves. After tasting and rating the chocolates, the students were offered a small box of the chocolates in lieu of cash as payment for their participation. I thought all college students would go for the cash, because I have a son in college and that's all he seems to need from me right now. Surprisingly, this study found that students faced with the smaller array of chocolates were four times more likely to accept the box of chocolates rather than the cash. They were also more satisfied with their tasting experience than those who tasted more varieties.

The authors of this study and other studies similar to it, according to Schwartz, hypothesize that:

> A large array of options may discourage consumers because it forces an increase in the effort that goes into making a decision. So consumers decide not to decide, and don't buy the product. Or if they do, the effort that the decision requires detracts from the enjoyment derived from the results. Also, a large array of options may diminish the attractiveness of what people actually choose . . . [because] thinking about the attractions of some of the unchosen options detracts from the pleasure derived from the chosen one.[1]

In today's world, technology and the Internet make access to information almost limitless. So as moms, how do we decide to decide and make good decisions? How do we stop the cycle of wondering if our decision was a good one?

What Kind of Decision Maker Are You?

First, determine your values. What's important to you as a mom? What goals do you have for your family? What do you hope to pass on to your children?

Once you have this sort of "big picture" in mind, this vision will guide you as you make other decisions. In *Momology: A Mom's Guide to Shaping Great Kids*, author Shelly Radic writes:

> I chose to focus my mothering on the end result, a picture of what I wanted my children to be like when they turned into big people. I took a holistic approach, desiring to influence my child's heart, soul, body, and mind. In my mind, I developed this big picture, filled with the things I deemed most important—things like faith, family, fun, respect, security, integrity, learning, and independence.[2]

I came across an idea that you might like to apply in your decision-making strategy. It's pretty simple, and it's from the book *The Paradox of Choice*. Schwartz describes two types of decision makers: maximizers and satisficers. (For the sake of this book and my aversion to spelling "satisficer," I'm going to refer to this type as "satisfiers.")

Maximizers seek and accept only the best.

Satisfiers settle for something good enough and do not worry about the possibility that there might be something better.

Maximizers want the very best. They want to feel assured that every decision they make is the best they could have made. Maximizers will spend enormous amounts of time and energy making a decision. For example, if a mom who is a maximizer wants to purchase a new car seat, she will check out all the alternatives. She'll visit all the local stores that sell car seats and compare prices. She will scour *Consumer Reports* and spend hours researching online. She'll talk to everyone she knows and hear which car seats her friends favor. Only after she feels certain she knows which is the best will she buy it. The problem is she will also continue to wonder if she really made the right decision. She'll continue to check options and may experience anxiety and regret after her decision.

A satisfier, on the other hand, will create standards and a list of criteria for decisions. She'll visit a few stores, ask a couple of friends, then search until she finds an item that meets those standards. Then she'll make her decision and stop. She won't agonize over it. She's not concerned about better options. She is confident with her decision.

In his book, Schwartz suggests that making decisions as a satisfier is a healthy practice. He conducted several different surveys of thousands of people, and after analyzing the data he writes, "Our expectation was confirmed. People with high maximization scores experienced less satisfaction with life, were less happy, less optimistic, and were more depressed than people with low maximization scores."[3] I think he's on to something. Choosing to limit your options when making a decision is wise.

However, this theory is easy for me to agree with because it is more natural for me. I was reminded by a good friend that sometimes I make decisions too quickly and could benefit from slowing myself down and considering more options. If you tend to make decisions quickly, consider researching a few more options to enhance your decision making.

Quiz: Are You a Maximizer or a Satisfier?

If you're not sure whether you're a maximizer or a satisfier, you can take this quiz below. Read each statement and decide if it is true or false for you.

_____ 1. Even though I'm pretty satisfied with my life, I often imagine how it could be better.

_____ 2. At a restaurant I have a difficult time deciding which dinner item to select, and after dinner I find myself wondering if I would have liked something else better.

_____ 3. I like to multitask online, and I always check out the links my friends post. I don't want to miss anything interesting.

_____ 4. I wait until the last minute at gift-giving times because I want to make sure that I've gotten the best possible gift for each person.

_____ 5. I like to check out all my options when I shop for myself, including online sales and multiple stores, but when I get home I still wonder if I've gotten the best deal.

_____ 6. My friends always ask me my opinion on restaurants, movies—you name it! I keep lists of the things I love.

_____ 7. I'd rather write an email than talk to someone on the phone because I want to make sure I have time to select the right words to convey my meaning.

_____ 8. Making major purchases for our family is difficult for me due to the number of choices and my

desire to get the highest quality and stay within our
budget.

____ 9. I set high standards for myself in most everything
I do.

____ 10. I often question my choices, wondering if I should
have decided differently.

You're done! Now, count the number of "true" answers
you had and the number you answered as "false." If you have
seven or more "true" answers then you're on the maximizer
end of the scale. If you had seven or more "false" answers,
you're more of a satisfier. If your answers were split evenly,
or close to even, you're probably somewhere in between.

Decision making takes lots of practice. Here are a few
suggestions to help simplify the sometimes overwhelming
process.

- Create your list of criteria and standards.
- Set limits for yourself. Limit the time you'll spend, the
options you'll consider, and the number of people you'll
chat with.
- Decide not to compare your choices to others'.
- Once you make a decision, don't look back.
- Eliminate excessively high expectations about the results
of your decisions.
- Embrace the unexpected.
- Allow yourself to make mistakes and learn from them.

There is nothing wrong with striving to make the best
decisions, but this style of decision making can help us make
quick, decisive decisions and feel confident with our choices.
At times we may decide to handle some choices differently.
If something is really important to us, we may spend a

significant amount of time researching and coming up with the best possible solution. But if we find ourselves bogged down on a specific decision and spending more time than we would like on it, then that might be a good indication to try some of the suggestions above.

Critical Thinking

Recently I was attending a writers' conference in Austin, Texas. One evening two other writers and I decided to venture out to see a phenomenon we had heard about. A local bridge was home to a huge colony of 700,000 bats! We walked down to the bridge, sat on a concrete wall, and waited until dusk, when the bats would come out of hiding and gobble up the bugs over the river. We ended up near two couples who were in their mid-twenties and were also waiting for the magic moment. One of the women started chatting with us. "Did you know they put bat poop in mascara?" she stated, as if it was a scientific fact.

"Really?" I said. "Are you sure?"

"Yeah, it's true. It's called guano and it's in some mascara. Gross, huh?"

"Wow, I'm going to have to check into that," I commented, thinking that sounded too farfetched for me to believe.

We watched the spectacle of hundreds of thousands of bats emerge from under the bridge and swoop around the sky, consuming the insects before moving slowly out of sight like a big dark cloud. Then we went back to our hotel. The gal at the bridge had piqued my curiosity. When I got to my room I did a little search on the Internet to see if mascara really contains bat poo. It didn't take long to find out the answer: No, it does not. Some mascara does contain a substance called guanine, but not guano. This young woman, like many of us, didn't think through the illogical rumor she had heard or read somewhere. As moms, without critical thinking skills we may believe certain suggestions or adopt the newest fads without logically thinking things through. And critical thinking needs to be part of all of our decision making, especially in today's world.

Critical thinking is the process of evaluating information and determining if it's true and relevant to our specific situations and needs. Karen Parks, director of strategic relationships for MOPS International, has worked with mothers of preschoolers for twenty-six years. She has a master's degree in reading, specializing in critical thinking. In speaking with me about this topic, she said, "I believe this current generation of moms has a challenge in the area of critical thinking because information is abundant on the Internet, and many people tend to believe what they read without questioning its validity."

She advises women to evaluate the source. "For example, if you find a site that says there is bat poop in mascara, take note of who sponsors that site. If it's a cosmetic company, then they might be making that claim to get you to buy their product rather than the other mascara at the drugstore."

Karen suggests three simple steps to help us include critical thinking in our decision-making method:

1. Be a skeptic. Think about who is telling you what, and why they might want you to agree with them or believe them.
2. Be informed. Ask smart questions. Also, have a few trusted resources and mentors to ask for advice. One good source that investigates Internet claims and urban legends and discovers if they are true or false is www .snopes.com.

3. Be an example to your kids. Developing critical thinking is a life skill to model and encourage in your children.

Do You Have the Courage to Trust Your Gut?

Sometimes in decision making, especially in the realm of parenting, a clear-cut answer is not easily found. Most times there is not one right answer. At those times trust your intuition—your unique MomSense—be in touch with your feelings, and listen to your thoughts and your emotional responses.

I began learning I could trust my MomSense when my middle son, Jordan, was twelve months old and became very sick. He wouldn't eat or drink anything, and he started to lose weight. We went to the doctor and they thought he just had a cold. He cried so much Zane and I had to literally take turns leaving the house so we could escape the sounds of his misery. A couple of days later Zane came down with a fever and sore throat. I knew what was wrong with Jordan! He had strep throat. I called our pediatrician and told her what was going on, and her answer baffled me.

"Babies don't get strep throat." End of conversation.

But I just knew in my gut he had strep throat. I called a different doctor and he agreed to see Jordan. After an exam he told me the same thing: "Babies just do not get strep throat." Neither doctor wanted to test him, because we were on the lowest-cost healthcare plan possible and they did not like to spend money on "needless" tests.

I submitted to their expertise and took Jordan home and tried to make him comfortable. This went on for ten days. Finally, I had enough. Jordan was pale, thin, worn-out, still not eating, and crying uncontrollably. I took him back to the first doctor.

Sitting across from me, she told me once again, "Babies don't get strep."

I looked her in the eyes and said, "I am not leaving your office until you test my baby for strep throat."

She huffed and shrugged her shoulders and said, "Okay, we'll give him the test."

Guess what? He did test positive for strep. By this point he was so sick he couldn't swallow the medicine. After trying a few times I had to take him back to the hospital where they gave him a shot filled with thick liquid into his thigh muscle. My heart hurt as I watched him cry while they massaged his leg to get the liquid to move into his system. It. Was. Awful.

I wished I had listened to my gut instinct sooner. My intuition was 100 percent correct. Today, Jordan is still a strep throat magnet, and I wonder if this experience has something to do with that. I can't go back and change what happened, but I did learn to trust my intuition.

If you don't feel a strong MomSense within yourself, talk to other moms! Trust others you respect, and seek their advice and opinions. Relying on each other's MomSense can also be a good strategy when facing a particular difficult predicament.

Mom Story

I Just Knew

I was a nineteen-year-old single mom when I had Cooper. The first day he wouldn't eat. I told the nurses he wasn't sucking, but they kept reminding me I was young and I just didn't know what was going on. But I knew something was wrong.

I kept telling the nurses Cooper wasn't eating until they finally believed me. But they didn't offer me much help or hope; instead they labeled him as a "failure to thrive" baby. I was devastated. It meant he might not survive and I didn't think there was anything I could do about it. I felt alone. The hospital was so full they had put me in the pediatric wing, probably because I was so young, so I wasn't even in the part of the hospital with other mommies and babies.

I took Cooper home and continued unsuccessfully to try to nurse him. I noticed his eyes were starting to sink into his head; he was listless and I was terrified. I asked my mom for help. She asked around and found a lactation specialist to meet with Cooper and me. This woman was a miracle worker. I met with her for an hour and she taught me how to nurse my baby. She did things like massage Cooper's tongue to get him to start sucking. It was amazing.

Thankfully I didn't accept the label put on my baby. My MomSense told me he could live, and I was right.

Brittany, mom of one

Listen to Your Feelings

In Jonah Lehrer's book *How We Decide,* he makes a good case for the idea that emotions play a vital role in decision making. He tells the story of a patient named Elliot who had a small brain tumor removed. Before the operation Elliot was a model father, husband, employee, and volunteer at his church. But the operation changed things. Elliot's IQ stayed the same, but after the surgery he was unable to make decisions. Everyday decisions such as what pen to use, what type of toothpaste to purchase, or what restaurant to go to for lunch literally took hours. Elliot's neurosurgeon decided to figure out what had happened.

After a series of tests, he found that Elliot was devoid of emotion. This was an astounding discovery, because at the time it was believed decision making was a very rational process and human emotions were irrational. As a result of Elliot's case, the theory that a person without emotions would make better decisions was tossed out the window, and the opposite was proved to be true. When a person loses the ability to feel, he or she is unable to make even the most commonplace decisions. "A brain that can't feel can't make up its mind," writes Lehrer.[4]

Other studies have confirmed the value of feelings in decision making. One study involved a group of female college students who were asked to select their favorite poster. They had five options: a Monet landscape, a van Gogh painting of some purple lilies, and three funny cat posters. Before choosing, they were divided into two groups. The first group was asked to simply rate each poster. The second group was given a questionnaire that asked them why they liked or disliked each of the five posters. When finished, each participant took her favorite poster home.

The results were fascinating. In the first group, 95 percent chose the fine art posters. But those who thought about their poster decisions first were equally split between the fine art and the funny cat posters. The researchers attributed this to the pressure they felt to articulate why they made their choice. It seemed easier to explain why a poster was funny rather than explain an unknown reason why purple flowers were interesting, so they chose the humorous cat poster.

A few weeks later researchers conducted follow-up interviews to see which group had made the better decision. Those in the first group were much more satisfied with their choice. But 75 percent of the women who chose the cat posters regretted their selection; nobody regretted selecting the artistic poster. "The women who listened to their emotions ended up making much better decisions than the women who relied on their reasoning powers. The more people thought about which posters they wanted, the more misleading their thoughts became. Self-analysis resulted in *less* self-awareness," writes Lehrer.[5]

After reading this I was very excited because moms feel— women feel! Sometimes we are the feelers of the family. Rather than discard a woman's emotional tendencies, this study validated the concept that feelings are an integral part of decision making.

Your MomSense is worth listening to; your MomSense matters! It's a precious exercise for each of us to discover our own MomSense, to combine what we learn with our gut feelings, and to grow in confidence, trusting what our instincts and education tell us to be true.

MomSense from Other Mothers

In our survey of five hundred moms, many stated they use both education and intuition in parenting decisions, but when asked to select one over the other, 83 percent said they relied more on intuition than education. Here's what some moms had to say:

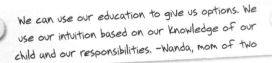

We can use our education to give us options. We use our intuition based on our knowledge of our child and our responsibilities. —Wanda, mom of two

I follow my gut and heart but occasionally need to rely on education and expert advice of another mom or professional. —Alice, mom of four

54

I have a master's degree and none of what I learned at the university prepared me for the struggles and challenges of being a mom. I rely on my personal experiences, help from friends and family, and listening to my child's unspoken needs to make the appropriate choices. -Lisa, mom of two

I rely more on my intuition, but I believe my education has shaped my intuition. -Karen, mom of two

I rely strongly on both, but since I do a lot of reading, I'll give the edge to education. I think education is my base and then intuition leads me from there. -Karen, mom of one

It really is a combination of intuition and education for me. When my son was younger it was a lot of education, but as he gets older I am trusting my intuition more. -Michelle, mom of one

Reject the Mommy Brain Stereotype!

Myth: When you become a mom you lose brain cells.
Truth: When you become a mom you become smarter.

In Katherine Ellison's book *The Mommy Brain: How Motherhood Makes Us Smarter*, she completely debunks the myth of mommies being airheaded, emotional wrecks. She cites study after study proving a woman's brain begins functioning at new levels once she becomes a mom. Some dormant parts of a woman's brain are activated by motherhood. We have much more going on in our heads than how to change a diaper and perform household chores. Moms are not ditzy, weeping piles of emotional messes, forgetting what we believe and losing the skills we developed prior to childbearing. In fact, according to Ellison, we literally do become smarter.

Expert Opinion

The Effects of Sleep Deprivation

The first few weeks of being a mommy are extremely exhausting. The lack of sleep due to a baby's needs will have an impact on any woman, making her feel crazy and inept at times. Remember, sleep deprivation is a form of torture and can make a woman do some crazy things. Effects of sleep deprivation include irritability, slower reaction times, diabetes, high blood pressure, depression, heart disease, and weight gain to name a few.[6]

I can't tell you how many times I put the milk in the pantry rather than the fridge, put mascara on one eye and forgot to do the other, or went to the grocery store with an unbuttoned shirt from a recent nursing session—wearing my fuzzy purple slippers.

One night after we brought our first baby home, I was more tired than I'd ever been in my life. I heard him crying and knew he needed to nurse. In my mind I got up, held him in my arms, and started nursing. The only problem was it was only in my mind. Zane got up to go get him and I said, "Don't worry, I've got him." I sat up in bed with my arms cradling a baby, only my arms were empty and Josh was still crying. My sweet husband must have thought I had lost it. I was crazy, but only temporarily. (Some of the best advice ever given to me was to sleep when the baby sleeps.)

For the first couple of months a mom moves into survival mode, taking care of a baby who needs constant attention and makes her sleep schedule erratic. But this is a temporary form of insanity. Remember, during this phase of having a baby your brain is learning—you *are* becoming smarter.

Ellison, after citing numerous studies that show a mommy brain is a smart brain, lists five attributes of a baby-boosted brain:

1. **Perception.** A mommy brain is expanding in the realm of senses. She senses when and what her baby needs. Her sense of smell and taste are heightened. "This is more than a matter of any of your five senses improving: You're paying attention and quickly learning from experience, because someone's life depends on it."[7]

2. **Efficiency.** Moms are masters of efficiency and grow in the ability to multitask. You know what I'm talking about: feeding a baby while at the same time talking on the phone and making a list of what to get at the grocery store. Or the story many of us have heard about the mom who's driving to work and using her breast pump at the same time. Need I say more?

3. **Resiliency.** Moms develop the skill of resilience. You are forced to, because your day is no longer a well-planned to-do list that you mostly control. You bounce from moment to moment, need to need, making constant adjustments as the day demands.

4. **Motivation.** Mothers can be the most motivated mammals on earth. Human mothers are no exception. The drive to love and care for other human beings ignites a ferocious desire in a woman to make the world a better place, if not for herself then definitely for her children.

5. **Emotional Intelligence.** Becoming a mother raises a woman's awareness and empathy for others.

The act of giving birth is many a woman's first real experience of utter loss of control. Bowled over by morning sickness, you can begin to imagine what it's like to be on chemotherapy. Pushed around in wheelchairs, you get a preview of what it's like to be old. Like a cult convert, ripped from the familiar trappings of your previous life, you drop your defenses and find yourself more open to the influence of others.[8]

Don't Be Afraid

Any woman can improve her ability to make a quick, decisive decision and feel confident about her choice. Consider intentionally limiting your choices, also known as "voluntary simplicity," when making a decision. Determine to only spend a specified amount of time researching your options. Limit the number of opinions you will seek.

And know it's okay to make mistakes. We are talented, educated, and highly motivated, and yet many of us hold an unspoken, perhaps unconscious, feeling that we should not make mistakes. But throughout history, people have always learned from mistakes. It's okay to make a mistake because we will grow from it. A friend of mine said, "You could do something wrong and fix it in the same time you could try to figure out how to do it perfect."

Everyone makes mistakes: you, me, the mom next door. No one has ever lived a mistake-free life. It's simply not possible. Live, make choices, make mistakes, make a different choice,

Expert Opinion

If you and your husband (or parenting partner) make decisions differently, you need to work very hard to come to a compromise or agreement that you both feel comfortable with. This may require a third party to help sort through the issues. If it is a minor issue (like whether or not the kids have to make their beds every day), compromise and be flexible. For major parenting decisions, like discipline, you need to both feel OK with the solution. Couples who communicate well (or have a mediator to help them do so) can almost always come to an agreement.

In a blended family situation, the biological parent should have "veto power" over parenting decisions (within reason).

Most importantly, the parents MUST be a united front to the kids. Disagreements need to be resolved away from their ears and the solution presented with mutual support.

Dr. Juli Slattery, family psychologist, Focus on the Family

and keep living a life without fear of failure. We can be bold in our decisions, embrace our mistakes, and continually grow into the moms we're meant to be.

So give it a try. Make a choice and then stop—and spend time coloring with your kiddos. (And don't get stuck with trying to decide what color crayon to use. Just grab one and have some fun.)

Your MomSense

- What is a decision you recently made?
- How did your final decision benefit from the work you put into it and the anxiety it caused you?
- If you could have a do-over, what would you do differently?
- Are you afraid of making a mistake in your mothering? Why or why not?
- Tell a mom friend about a recent mistake you made. (Don't be surprised if she says "me too.")
- Are you a maximizer or a satisfier?
- What can you do to voluntarily limit your range of options in the choices you make?

Discovering Your MomSense Section Summary

Hopefully, we have discovered more about our own Mom-Sense. Each of us might have developed a personal definition of MomSense: how to apply common sense to mothering, what we bring into our role as mom based on childhood experiences, and what strengths and weaknesses we possess. Many of us may have discovered more about our individual decision-making tendencies and perhaps gained ideas to help make future good choices that affect others. Most of all, I hope we've realized that what we've discovered about our own unique MomSense doesn't end here but is a lifetime of learning.

Now it's time to use our MomSense and create a mothering philosophy based on key foundational principles that can help guide us on this journey of motherhood.

Section 2

Practicing Your MomSense

prac·tice *a*: to perform or work at repeat-
edly so as to become proficient
b: to train by repeated exercises

Every woman who becomes a mother has to begin learning how to mother. And just like any other activity in life, mothering is a skill that takes practice.

Because all moms need practice to improve their mothering skills, I always feel a little sorry for all firstborn children. They are the ones we usually have to experiment the most on. They become the firsts of so many experiences:

- first diaper
- first sick baby
- first teething experience

- first to ride a bike
- first to make discipline decisions about

- first to make school decisions about
- first to be teenagers
- first to drive a car
- first to have a date

- first to leave the home (I know, I know, don't even go there)
- and so much more

But we all begin somewhere. Zane and I have found ourselves telling our first child, Josh, that we're learning too. We've had to learn and adjust our parenting as he's grown older and as we've had more children. One big thing we've learned is that we had to adjust what we thought was working for each child depending on his temperament. With each child I have grown more confident, but I've also had to keep my mind constantly open to changing and readjusting my parenting strategies, figuring out what works best for each one.

Mom Story

Parenting Multiple Personalities

My first baby was on a perfect schedule. Sleep, eat, play, sleep. *What is the big deal?* I wondered, listening to other moms talk about how hard it was to get their baby on a schedule. Three years later I finally understood. I couldn't get my second baby scheduled if my life depended on it. I did everything by the book, just as I had with my first child, yet none of it worked.

Now, a decade later, I look back at my baby scheduling experiences and realize that the temperament differences between these two children of mine are still true today in their teenage years. As a mom, it's my job to know their bents, their hard wiring, their gifts and talents, and to remind them of who they are as they traverse through life.

For example, I am not going to point my creative daughter toward a world of math and analytics. That would squelch her. Instead, I point her toward her love for creative writing and passion for social justice.

Parenting into the individuality of our children is a richly rewarding challenge as we learn to celebrate and appreciate their uniqueness and fan the flame of how they were uniquely created.

Laura, mom of three

Current research also shows that most women want to be better moms and are hungry for information to help improve their mothering skills. Endless lists exist on basic mothering skills, so for the sake of creating a book that actually ends, I've looked at lots of these lists and developed this section based on common themes I found. We'll look at the following and discover practical tips and tools on how to develop these essential elements for successful mothering:

- **Sense of Patience.** Intentionally practicing patience: the ability to endure waiting, delay, or provocation without becoming annoyed or upset.
- **Sense of Respect.** Modeling and teaching the Golden Rule: do unto others as you would have them do unto you.
- **Sense of Consistency.** Becoming the reliable, faithful mom your children need.
- **Sense of Perspective.** Avoiding the nonsense and focusing on what matters most.
- **Sense of Self-Control.** Practicing and modeling self-discipline in a self-indulgent world.
- **Sense of Calm.** Remaining composed in the chaos and creating a peaceful home.

- **Sense of Joy.** Maintaining a sense of humor and creating a joyful atmosphere in the home.
- **Sense of Love.** Building a sensible mothering philosophy grounded in unconditional love.

As we've discovered, mothering may come a little easier for some women than for others—just like some people are natural-born runners or piano players but others have to work hard to develop these skills. But in any case, to get better at running or piano playing or mothering, we need to practice. And with practice anyone can improve her MomSense and become a better mom.

4

Sense of Patience

Patience is not passive; on the contrary, it
is active, it is concentrated strength.

Edward G. Bulwer-Lytton

Pa·tient *(adj)* **1:** bearing pains or trials calmly without
complaint **2:** manifesting forbearance under provocation or strain **3:** not hasty or impetuous **4:** stead-
fast despite opposition, difficulty or adversity[1]

Ugh. Patience is not one of my virtues. I get frustrated with
slow drivers, slow sales clerks, slow decision makers, slow
employees at fast food restaurants—and especially slow kids!

I remember one day when I caught myself ranting as I rushed
my kids, ages eight, five, and three, out the door to get somewhere on time. Feeling really angry and impatient, I knew my

"hurry-ups" were getting louder and louder, and I could feel my teeth clenching as I became more and more frustrated. As my littlest one scurried through the door, he looked up at me and what I saw stopped me cold. My child's eyes were filled with fear. You'd have thought he was looking at a monster. And I was that monster—the impatient, hurry-up monster.

The very next day, I decided to try something new. I promised myself that I would not say "hurry up" for an entire day, to practice being patient. It did not come easily to me. My husband was out of town so I was on my own, but I was determined to conquer the hurry-up monster once and for all. Here's what happened:

6:30 a.m. In preparation for the battle ahead, I memorized Proverbs 10:19, "When words are many, sin is not absent, but he who holds his tongue is wise."

6:45 a.m. Time to wake the kids. I pulled their covers down and tempted them with talk of Fruit Loops and cinnamon toast.

7:00 a.m. I headed back to check the kids' progress. They were playing with toys and still in their pajamas. Fruit Loops were soggy and soaking in a sea of pink milk. Toast was cold. Already, I had to bite my tongue as the words "hurry up" tried to escape my lips.

7:45 a.m. Time to head out the door. All three boys were fed and mostly dressed. The little ones didn't have their shoes on, but I decided to come home after dropping Josh at school instead of running our usual errands, so bare feet were okay. I thought I could win this battle if I did as little as possible that day. Using my sweetest tone of voice, I said, "I'm getting in the car."

7:55 a.m. I sat in the car with my two little ones waiting for my eight year old to join me. The temptation to holler "hurry up" grew greater by the minute, but I actively willed myself not to say it.

8:45 a.m. My two younger boys and I took a walk to the creek near our home.

9:20 a.m. I had a phone meeting at ten and I knew how slow my three and five year olds could be. I decided to start the short walk home.

9:48 a.m. In 28 minutes, we had only made it one block. The boys stopped to pick up every stick and look at every bug that crossed our path. The five year old's pants were slipping because his pockets were weighted down with all the rocks he had gathered. It took a lot of patience for me not to hurry them along, but I was beginning to see the rewards of winning this battle. The boys were completely relaxed and thoroughly enjoying themselves, and I had slowed down enough to enjoy watching them play.

11:30 a.m. Time for lunch. It's amazing how long it takes two kids to eat peanut butter and honey sandwiches when they aren't being told to hurry.

12:30 p.m. I dropped off my three year old at a friend's house so I could go to his brother's preschool party. With only one child to contend with, I figured not hurrying would be a breeze.

12:45 p.m. We left the house fifteen minutes early to return a movie to the video store. I let my son put the movie in the drop box. Normally, I would tell him to run to the box and jump quickly back in the car. This time I didn't rush him, and we barely made it to the party on time. I realized, however, that no one would even have noticed if we'd showed up at preschool a few minutes late.

2:30 p.m. After the party, I waited to see how long it took for my son to put his seatbelt on without being rushed.

2:34 p.m. Finally, I heard the seatbelt click. A five year old can't do two things at once, and he was busy telling me about a game he and his friend had played. Normally, I might have interrupted his story and impatiently reminded him to get his seatbelt on so we could leave. But I actually enjoyed sitting in the car listening to his story.

2:45 p.m. I picked up my oldest from school and went to pick up the youngest. I let the kids play while I visited with my friend. Getting the kids back into the car without saying "hurry up" was painful.

3:30 p.m. Time for homework. I let the younger boys watch a cartoon so they wouldn't distract their brother—and so I wouldn't cave in and lose the battle that I seemed to be winning so far.

4:30 p.m. I decided on frozen pizza for dinner, something simple because we needed to get to my oldest son's baseball game by 5:15. I began to gear myself up mentally for the challenge of not saying "hurry up" to make it to the game on time.

5:00 p.m. As we drove to the baseball game, my oldest son hollered from the backseat, "Mom, pass that slow car; we're going to be late!" The truth hit me hard. I'd taught my kids to be impatient, just like me.

7:30 p.m. Time for bed. This, by far, was the hardest part of my day. Not saying "hurry up" to three boys getting ready for bed is like not saying "ouch," or some other four-letter word, when you stub your toe. The boys put on their pajamas while I put toothpaste on their toothbrushes and set them next to the sink.

8:00 p.m. Toothpaste starting to harden on toothbrushes.

8:15 p.m. I decided to forget about brushing teeth and began our story reading ritual. Overcoming my natural tendencies, I vowed not to read too fast, not to skip any pages, and not to shorten any of Dr. Seuss's long tongue twisters.

8:30 p.m. Middle son reminds everyone they haven't brushed their teeth. Dang it!

8:40 p.m. Pray (hard) for a little more patience to finish the day well.

8:45 p.m. Forty-five minutes later than usual, all the boys are tucked peacefully in bed.

8:50 p.m. My three year old complained that we forgot to pray he wouldn't have that dream about the bad pirate who tried to take his favorite stuffed tiger away from him.

8:51 p.m. Prayed that the bad pirate wouldn't take my son's stuffed tiger from him.

9:00 p.m. Exhausted, I tucked myself into bed, but I experienced a sense of satisfaction. I had spent an entire day without saying "hurry up" out loud and was a better mom for it. I realized it would be harder for the hurry-up monster to haunt our home again.[2]

I grew a bit in patience that day and saw the benefits of this virtue for me and my kids—and also realized practicing patience is hard work. It's like making yourself get up at five a.m. and run ten miles every day for two weeks, but becoming a patient mommy enhances our MomSense, helping us become the moms we crave to be.

Patience is a huge challenge for almost every mom. For some reason children bring our lack of patience (which most of us have) to the forefront. Just when I think I've got myself under control and I haven't lost my patience for a while, something will set me off. A few months ago, I was so tired of seeing the boys' shoes, tee shirts, socks (usually just one sock, who knows where the other is), lacrosse balls, bouncy balls, basketballs, soccer balls, coats, hats, mittens, backpacks, papers, and a myriad of other stuff all over the floor near the front door, I just lost it. I had asked them several times to pick their stuff up and put it away, but that wasn't the top item on their to-do lists. So I huffed, and snatched it all up in my arms and threw it outside. When the boys started looking for an item, like their shoes, guess whom they asked first. Mom. "It's outside," I coolly responded.

Unfortunately, they found this hysterical. Now when they can't find their shoes, they ask me, "Mom, did you freak out again and throw my stuff outside?"

MomSense from Other Mothers

What causes you to really lose your patience with your kiddos?

Disobedience and ridiculous messiness.
—Christine, mom of three

When my kids put their dirty clothes on the clean clothes pile that they never put away. Or, next to the dirty clothes hamper! Why not in it? I don't get it. —Jill, mom of four

I hate fussy eaters! My almost-four year old is the worst I've ever seen! Drives us insane! —Laura, mom of two

When he doesn't listen after I tell him something 2,349,823,749,283 times! —Krystal, mom of one

WHINING! —Marcia, mom of two

When my kids play fighting turns into real full-on fist fights. Happens every day! The worst is in the car. I have a Suburban but even that doesn't keep them far enough apart. —Jenn, mom of four

Patience is something that anyone can lose, but fortunately, anyone can find it again. I lost my patience when I threw the boys' stuff outside. And believe me, that is not the only moment I've lost it. I'm sure there are hundreds of effective ways to get my boys to pick up after themselves. But my patience had evaporated. However, after that moment of losing my cool I had another moment to get it back, and to practice patience again and again and again.

Tips to Help You Radiate Cool

1. Know if you're tired. When a person is tired her reserve of patience runs thin. If you're tired, give yourself a time-out.
2. Do an attitude check. Are you a perfectionist? Do you have unrealistic expectations of your children? Do you need to let go of some of the demands you're putting on yourself and your children?
3. PMS. Know your menstrual cycle. It's very common for women to experience less patience during certain times of the month.
4. Be aware of your stress level. People under intense stress lose their patience quickly.
5. Employ your sense of humor. Many moments that can cause a mom to lose her patience can actually be quite funny, if you stop and think about it.
6. Did you grow up in a home with a parent who had a short fuse? If so, be aware of your own tendency to model what you grew up with.
7. Remember your children are watching you. If you want patient children you need to try to be a patient adult. But we all lose it, and learning to say "I'm sorry" is good for everyone.

Mom Story

Just in Time

I sat at my computer trying to do some emails for work while Eva played on the floor nearby. She kept asking me questions, interrupting my train of thought, and I could feel my patience with her running out. I really needed to get some work done today. Then I had an idea. I went to my kitchen and grabbed my timer.

"Eva, Mommy really needs to get some work done, so I'm going to set this timer for ten minutes. I want you to play alone in your room while I work, then after ten minutes I'm all yours."

This worked for us. It became kind of a game. I was able to work and Eva knew after the timer went off she would have my full attention. She looks forward to hearing the buzz of the timer, indicating the end of my work time. Then she runs into my office and we play.

I even began to set the timer for more time when needed, and she's learned to entertain herself for longer.

Jacque, mom of two

Your MomSense

- Would you describe yourself as patient? Why or why not?
- What is something you can do for a single day to practice patience with your children?
- What are some recognizable signals that indicate you're about to lose your patience?
- When you recognize those signals, what can you do to intentionally practice patience?

5

Sense of Respect

Do to others as you would have them do to you.

Luke 6:31

Imagine the following two scenes.

Scene One: Two moms enter a movie theater, enjoying some time together.

Mom One: "I need to run into the restroom. I'll be right back."

Mom Two: "Okay, I'll go buy some popcorn and a couple sodas and meet you right back here."

Scene Two: Mom Two with her two-year-old son at the public library. They just sat down on the carpet in front of the volunteer who reads stories every week to the kids.

Little Boy: "Mom, I need to go potty."

Mom Two: "Again? You're kidding me! Why didn't you go before we got here! Just try to hold it for a while."

Little Boy: "Mommy, I can't hold it. I need to go now." He wiggles around struggling to control his urge to go potty.

Mom Two: Grabs her son roughly by the arm. "Alright, let's go, but hurry up! Story time is about to start."

Respect sounds easy, but for some reason it is difficult when it comes to our own families. However, a mom with good MomSense will both give respect and model respectful behavior to others. In the scenes above, wouldn't it be odd for the mom to talk to her friend the way in which she spoke to her little boy? Even rude, ignorant, or socially awkward people wouldn't get angry with a friend for needing to use the bathroom. I know, because I'm the woman who needs to go even if I just *see* the word "restroom." (I'm not saying I have rude, socially awkward friends, but if I did . . .)

> Respect = Treating others as you would have others treat you.

My friends never get frustrated with me. They respect my need to relieve myself. It's no big deal.

But, sadly, it's not that unusual to see a mother give her child a little yank and use angry words because of a seemingly insignificant incident. Maybe it is the hundredth time that hour he's had to go potty. Maybe the mom is pregnant, and getting in and out of those stalls in public places is horribly awkward and inconvenient. Maybe it's going to make the family late for an appointment. Believe me, I know. I've been that mom. But no matter the reason, we need to practice treating our own families as we want to be treated—and as we want them to treat others.

We as moms can set the example, beginning with our own children. A mom with good sense possesses and exhibits respect.

If you were raised in a home where you were not treated with respect, growing this part of your MomSense may be more of a struggle for you. But we all have the opportunity to break a cycle of behavior. Our actions, words, and attitudes will rub off on our children, making it easier for them to be respectful to us, family members, and others. The impact will be felt on future generations.

Respect is a little seven-letter word with HUGE meaning. To be respectful means to be:

• kind	• honoring	• patient
• honest	• dignifying	• supportive
• compassionate	• courteous	• gracious
• considerate	• good	• grateful
• admiring	• gentle	• understanding
• esteeming	• loving	• caring
• valuing	• appreciative	• uplifting

Respect is not:

• demeaning	• rude	• critical
• degrading	• dominating	• mocking
• humiliating	• conceited	• insulting
• ashamed	• selfish	

Developing Respectful Children

If we want to raise respectful children, we have to be respectful adults.

When I received my master's degree in journalism, my thesis was about television's portrayal of family life. I did lots of research on whether or not children model what they see on television. Turns out they do. Duh. But one theory I came across in my research is called the Social Learning

Theory. This theory, which numerous studies support, states that the number one method of learning behavior is through observing real live people. Double duh. (The second is TV, because it is close to real live people.)

I truly believe we have to live the life we want our kids to live and be the kind of person we want our children to be, because they do copy what they see in us. Especially when it comes down to using our MomSense in the dailies. How we live daily, what attitudes we exhibit, and how we treat others is imprinted on the brains and hearts of the little people around us.

Even though we are the adults in the family, do look for opportunities to learn from your children.

With All Due Respect

Tips to Help Raise Respectful Kids

- **Interact often with your children.** They will feel cherished if you spend time with them. Not just "let's all sit around the TV" time, but time where you practice cooperating, communicating, and getting to know each other.
- **Value your children's thoughts and opinions.** For example, if a child expresses embarrassment when you brag about them to others, or ask them to perform a skill in front of others, then don't do that anymore. Respect their feelings.
- **Say nice things about other people.** Make it a habit to compliment others, even someone you meet for a moment. If you say negative things about others your children will do that too.
- **Use positive forms of communication.** As Mother Teresa said, "Kind words can be short and easy to speak but their echoes are endless." Avoid raising your voice or using condescending words. Do be cheerful and positive.
- **Do what you say.** Your children will respect you if you consistently do what you say, and they will learn the value of being a person of integrity.
- **When (not if) you mess up, say "I'm sorry."** We will make mistakes. Apologizing will earn you more respect than trying to prove you were right. And your children will mess up too. Encourage and accept their apologies.

Mom Story

Be Kind

As I braked, I glanced at my daughter in the rearview mirror; it was already too late to distract her.

"Mom, that man lost his job and his home and he's hungry and anything helps. That makes me so sad!" Katie started crying before she could finish talking.

I took a deep breath and plunged into another challenging parenting moment. We'd had a long day already. She was tired. I was ready to put a frozen pizza in the oven, begin jammie time, and plop onto the futon.

"Oh, the man by the road there? Is that what his sign said?" I feigned ignorance. I didn't want to talk about this now. "That *is* sad. Does it make you feel any other way?"

"No, I just want to cry for a while."

I gave her a few minutes to process her feelings and thought through my response. On a selfish level, I knew that if we left the conversation there, I would have a difficult time getting her to stop crying at bedtime. But on a mothering level, I wanted her to take charge of her feelings and take a small step toward growing up. And I suppose I also wanted to pay a little penance for the cynicism I held toward "beggars."

With only a few miles before home, I reached back to hold her hand and asked if she wanted to talk.

"I understand how sad it made you to think about that man not having a home and a job. It makes me sad too, but I'm also very thankful that

Daddy and I have jobs and we have a nice warm home
to live in."

"And we can buy groceries." She was just snif-
fling now.

I passed our street and drove around the block.
I figured we should talk it through to the end.

"And you know it's okay to be sad sometimes.
But you don't want to be sad all the time, do
you?"

"No, I wouldn't like that." She wiped a few
tears and boogers away with her sleeve.

"That's why when I'm sad about something, I try
to stop and think about why I'm sad, but I don't
stop there. I try to figure out how to let my sadness turn into an action. What do you think we
could do to help people like that man?"

"We could give them food, like apples and
stuff, and we could give them things like blankets
and soap."

"Those are great ideas! Next time we go to the
store together, let's get an extra box of granola
bars and maybe some soap. Then when we see someone
who's hungry, we'll have something to give them," I
said.

Elsa, mom of two

Many times our children are examples to us of what it means to treat others respectfully. The innocent heart and untainted attitude of her daughter toward a man who was homeless and hungry impacted Elsa. It motivated her to actually go to the store and keep food and soap in her car for the next time she saw a homeless person. If Elsa had hardened her heart or ignored her daughter, this little incident probably would have been forgotten. But instead she used this moment to take an action. She listened to her daughter and

Expert Opinion

Actions Do Speak Louder Than Words

One of the simplest and most important secrets of real mothering is recognizing that kids learn by watching and listening. So be careful, Mom. Our children see how we react to stress, and they mimic our example. They hear how we speak to (or about) our friends, and they talk the same way to their peers. They tune in to what makes us tear up or become angry or soften, and they mimic. Our kids learn patience or impatience, compassion or indifference, tolerance or prejudice, frugality or materialism through our daily example. It's such a simple secret, but one too often overlooked. We just plain fail to realize how influential we can be in our children's lives. Maybe it's because we are all too caught up in this modern motherhood misconception that the other stuff (the doing, the going, the activities) is what's crucial. Slow down Mom: *don't undermine your influence.* Your everyday example is a living textbook to your children. What you model to your child in those little everyday unplanned moments can be far more important than all the flash cards, carpools, computer games and tutoring.[1]

Michele Borba, EdD, recipient of the National Educator Award, author and speaker

helped meet some needs of others all thanks to the honest tears of a kindergartner.

A mom with good MomSense practices respect everywhere. Jesus knew what he was talking about when he suggested we treat others as we want to be treated. The beautiful concept behind respect is you do get what you give.

MomSense from Other Mothers

How do you encourage respect in your home life?

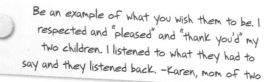

Be an example of what you wish them to be. I respected and "pleased" and "thank you'd" my two children. I listened to what they had to say and they listened back. —Karen, mom of two

I always believe that respect for people starts with respect for other living things. My son has his own plant in his bedroom that he takes responsibility for and he shows great respect for it, even giving it a name and talking to it! Feeding the birds, not squishing bugs, stuff like that, is a great way of encouraging respect. From this comes a respect for humans, I'm hoping. –Hazel, mom of one

We're careful about joking around. There's a balance between laughing with someone and laughing at someone. Laughing at someone is not respectful, and so we emphasize that in our home. –Terry, mom of three

One time I was chopping celery and halfway listening to my son. He grabbed my hand, looked up at me, and asked me to listen to him with both ears. So now, I try to listen to my children with both ears, use eye contact, and value their thoughts, ideas, and opinions. –Jeanne, mom of three

Your MomSense

- Describe actions that are respectful.
- Describe actions that are disrespectful.
- What does or would respect look like in your home?
- What is one thing you can do today to show your children you respect others?
- What is one thing you can do today to show your children you have respect for them?

6

Sense of Consistency

> If you are calm, you are consistent, and you always do what you say you're going to, you will earn their (your children's) respect and trust.
>
> *Dr. Kevin Leman*[1]

Melissa collapsed onto her bed, barely able to keep her eyes open. It had been a long day and she was exhausted. Her husband traveled, so most nights she conducted the bedtime routine of reading, praying, and tucking her two little girls in for the night alone. Recently, her strong-willed, six-year-old daughter Lauren would not stay in her bed.

Tonight was no different. As Melissa drifted in and out of consciousness she heard the little pitter-patter of Lauren's feet shuffling toward her bedroom. *Oh please, not tonight,* Melissa pleaded. Then a tap on her door.

"Mommy," Lauren whispered. "I'm thirsty."

"Lauren, Mommy already gave you a drink. It's time for bed," Melissa said.

She heard Lauren sigh and knew she was still standing by her door, thinking of some other excuse to not go to bed. This was becoming a battle of wills and Melissa didn't want to lose. She couldn't go night after night taking an hour or two before Lauren finally stayed in her bed and slept. Melissa had already given in several nights in a row because she didn't have the energy to do what she knew she needed to do.

Tonight, although exhausted, Melissa resolved to stick to her guns and stop this crazy cycle. She had recently read in a parenting book to put your child to bed and basically ignore them until the next day. *Now or never*, Melissa thought. She got up, held Lauren's hand, walked her to her bedroom, gave her a hug and kiss goodnight, and said, "Lauren, Mommy is tired and I'm going to bed. I've said my goodnights to you and now I'm not going to talk to you until tomorrow morning. I love you." She turned around and walked away, determined to do what she had said.

A few minutes later Lauren was knocking on her door again and calling out to her, but this time Melissa ignored her. She knew Lauren was safe. Soon, her daughter's knocking turned into pounding and her cries for "Mommy" grew louder. "Mommy, talk to me," she demanded. This persistent little girl knew her mom had given in before and would probably give in again.

But Melissa didn't.

After about twenty minutes of this behavior, Lauren stopped. *Finally*, Melissa thought. *I can't take much more.* Then Melissa heard the whirr of the vacuum cleaner that she had left in the living room earlier that day. *What in the world? She's fired up the vacuum to get my attention.* Melissa wanted to both scream and laugh at the absurdity of the situation. *Well, I'll just let her keep vacuuming, and I'll have really clean rugs tomorrow,* Melissa coached herself, trying to find a positive in the situation. Then the vacuum cleaner went off and the house was silent. Melissa waited about twenty more minutes before peeking into her daughter's room. Lauren was sound asleep. After one more night of ignoring Lauren's attempts to not go to bed, this pattern of behavior stopped. Melissa followed through and did what she said she was going to do. Although it wasn't easy, it worked.

Being true to our word as moms is hard work.

I admire Melissa's ability to do what she said and not get up and give in to her daughter's demands. But it was hard. In parenting it's so much easier to avoid the battles, but then the battles continue and can become more serious, creating kids who make demands and expect those demands to be met.

These types of situations, with children testing our resolve to follow through on what we say, occur over and over during our parenting years. We might as well learn to practice faithful, consistent parenting while our children are young, so they will know we mean what we say.

MomSense from Other Mothers

What advice would you give to other moms about being consistent?

It's hard in the beginning but it pays off in the end. —Sabrina, mom of one

Consistency is the best bet, but be sure to pick your battles if you need to cave in once in awhile. —Laura, mom of two

Don't sweat the small stuff. If you discipline over every single thing your voice becomes a constant background drone! Mean business when you need to. –Julie, mom of two

Mom Story
You Said He Couldn't Do What for How Long?

I had been a single mom for five years before falling in love and marrying Will. He's a wonderful man and father to my son, Cooper, but inexperienced as a dad. I had done this parenting gig alone for a while and now we were trying to do it together.

One night, when I was out with friends, Will tried to put Cooper to bed and Cooper refused to put on his jammies. So, Will said, "Okay, no going to the park for the next week."

When I got home and Will told me the consequences he had set for Cooper's disobedience I was frustrated. I'm the one who would be with him most of the time for the following week, and not going to the park for seven whole days was going to be much harder on me than on Cooper. The park is just behind our home. We can see it from our back patio, and we go there all the time when I know Cooper needs to get outside and play. It would have been better if Will would have said he couldn't go to the park for a day or two, but a whole week? Anyway, I told Will I would support him in this decision.

Then a couple of days later, I went to the store and left Cooper with Will. When I came home

I looked out the back window and saw Cooper at
the park playing with his neighborhood friends. I
asked Will why he let him go when we had decided he
couldn't go for a week, and Will said, "I felt bad
for him looking out the window and not being able
to go and play with his friends. I let him go."

Will is a softy and we laughed about this. We
also learned a little about setting consequences
that are realistic and not harder on us than on
Cooper.

Brittany, mom of one

Being a faithful, consistent mom is very important, not only for a mom's sanity but also for the child to know he can depend on his mom. A child needs to know his mom will follow through on what she says in regard to discipline and in so many other ways, such as following through with promised activities, faithfully picking him up on time from play dates, or consistently remaining calm in unexpected situations. This shows a child his mom is faithful, someone he can rely on. A mom growing in her MomSense will see how being consistent in many areas of life will help her build her parenting skills.

Your MomSense

- Describe a time when it was difficult for you to be consistent in a parenting situation:

- How did your child respond to you?
- Share with other moms any struggles you have regarding consistency in your parenting practice, and ask a good friend to check in on this with you regularly to see if you're getting better at following through.

7

Sense of Perspective

For those who have seen the earth from space, and for the hundreds and perhaps thousands more who will, the experience most certainly changes your perspective. The things that we share in our world are far more valuable than those which divide us.

Donald Williams, astronaut

Jordan walked out of his room wearing his new green and gray plaid shorts and his favorite purple- and yellow-striped polo shirt—a fashion disaster according to rules of style and color coordination but not according to Jordan, who, by the way, is color blind. He smiled at me, proud of his bright colors, his new clothes, and his ability to get himself dressed. He had no clue it didn't match, and of course he didn't care.

So why did I care? Maybe it's because I look at too many magazines showing adorable kids in their matching clothes, or walk through too many malls and admire the children's clothing displays, or because all of my friends' children always look so charming.

I'm sure my upbringing and lessons in how to dress for success play a role in my fashion expectations for my children. Whatever the reason, I had to bite my tongue to keep from asking him to go change his clothes and squelch the urge I felt to take his hand, walk him back into his bedroom, open his drawers, pull out the solid green shirt I bought to go with those plaid shorts, and then somehow bribe him into wearing it. But as I looked at him and saw his big, bright, chocolate-brown eyes and his sweet smile, I chose not to care. Besides, he looked adorable in all those colors.

I had a change in my perspective. My MomSense kicked in and my self-sense kicked out. I made a conscious choice to let Jordan be Jordan and not worry if his clothes matched or not. I know this is a minor life issue, but it sticks in my mind as a moment where I changed my point of view.

I decided colors don't clash. Just ask God. All of creation is filled with beautiful, vibrant colors all mixed together—colors that take your breath away. So I decided to let my kids wear colorful clothes, whether they matched or not. But more importantly, I decided looking good on the inside mattered most.

The pressure to look perfect begins at an early age. As a mom I want to make sure my children know that what matters most is on the inside, not what they wear on the outside. First Samuel 16:7 says, "Man looks at the outward appearance, but the LORD looks at the heart." So the next time Jordan came down the stairs in his purple shirt and plaid green shorts with his Batman cape looped around his shoulders, mismatched socks, and snow boots, I took his hand in mine and said, "Let's go."

Gaining a healthy perspective in life helps us recognize what matters and what doesn't. A mom with good MomSense will acquire a healthy perspective, keeping in mind what really does matter in her own big picture.

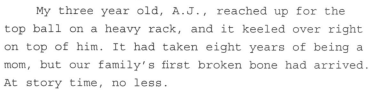

Mom Story

Then and Now

I saw it coming.

My three year old, A.J., reached up for the top ball on a heavy rack, and it keeled over right on top of him. It had taken eight years of being a mom, but our family's first broken bone had arrived. At story time, no less.

Eight years ago, as a new mom, I would have convened a committee to decide if I should take a child to the emergency room. But now, I arranged for a friend to take my middle son home and I calmly took off for the hospital with A.J. It was almost surreal how peaceful the experience was. Yes, he was in constant pain. Yes, I had four interviews scheduled that day for an article I was writing. But something took over.

I knew to ask that A.J. get his own turn with a stethoscope. I helped turn his bed into a magic choo-choo on the way to radiology. I thought to ask that he be able to see his own x-ray, and to explain to him how some people grow up to be nurses and doctors. They gave him a little bear. I made it a sling to match his. I knew just where to rub his head. I knew when to ask the doctor a question and when to just listen.

I suddenly flashed back to 3½ years earlier, when I was staring into a plastic box at the same boy at 2 pounds, 7 ounces, tubed up to kingdom come. Every beep made me *crazy*. Every doctor visit, I had a million questions that, as soon as I asked, I would forget the answers to. A.J. spent 46 scary, beautiful days in the NICU that became my entire existence.

So it was startling to see A.J. in a hospital bed again, the big kind, asking me if he could keep his hospital gown. The spirit of my youngest child has always amazed me. But on this day I guess I amazed me too, that I could actually see a broken clavicle as quite manageable and show that to my hurting son. Maybe because that same collarbone used to be smaller than my wrist.

This time, the gift of mothering perspective came as I remembered our early hospital days, when A.J. wore credit-card-sized diapers and oxygen tubes sprouted from everywhere on his teeny body. How far we've come. How far *I've* come.

Susan, mom of three

The NonSense

It makes me sad to read and hear about the "Mommy Wars," different issues that divide mothers such as breast-feeding versus bottle-feeding, stay-at-home mom versus working mom, public school versus home school, and cloth versus disposable diapers. But I think these "wars" are partly due to the media's interest in dramatizing different opinions into divisive issues. Whenever I talk to moms, I don't sense this warlike attitude.

Most moms I come across are pretty reasonable. Most moms I meet express feeling a bond the moment they meet another mom. They do acknowledge parenting differences, but they also seem to accept and not judge those who parent differently. So what's all this talk about "Mommy Wars"? Let's put this nonsense behind us and focus on what we share in common, befriend those with differences, and see how this expands our own world—and perhaps even changes our own perspective. Let's show the world that we are more mature than the media makes us out to be.

I think the bigger issue is when the nonsense becomes personal. We can easily get sucked into some type of MomSense NonSense, such as:

Comparing. Women tend to compare themselves to others and we just need to stop. I like what Eleanor Roosevelt said: "No one can make you feel insecure without your consent."

Judging. Psychiatryze [sigh-kigh-uh-try-zz]. This is a word my twenty-one-year-old niece came up with and posted on Facebook. She defined it as "prematurely psychologically analyzing and diagnosing individuals." I totally know what she means. I know I've judged people prematurely, and others have done the same to me. We think we've got others figured out and so many times we're just plain wrong. Consider others with a nonjudgmental attitude. We have so much to offer each other.

Busyness. It's easy to get sucked into the idea that being busy is somehow equated with being important. And it's easy to think everyone should be just as busy, pulling the same weight as us. Let's give each other the freedom to determine our own schedules and commitments, and respect that each person's "busyness meter" maxes out at different levels.

Bossiness. Sometimes people find an issue that becomes passionately important to them, such as eating natural food, using cloth diapers, or never letting their daughters play with Barbies. That is fine for each individual, but it becomes a problem when that person tries to convince everyone else to see things the same way. Let's continue to work on accepting differences while maintaining our own convictions with a sense of humbleness and grace.

Mom Story

Picking a Preschool

The decision about which preschool would be best for my firstborn was a huge stress for me. I agonized about making the right decision and wanted "the best" for my son. This quest for the perfect preschool became nonsense as I visited schools and compared programs.

I loved a preschool near our home that was associated with a university and had small class sizes, an amazing new building, enriching activities, and a highly regarded curriculum. After visiting that "top-line" school, nothing else seemed to measure up.

Then I got a moment of reality and understood that it truly was nonsense to spend the equivalent of college tuition on preschool for a three year old. It was crazy to think I would have to go back to work to afford the tuition. It was preschool, not Harvard, for goodness sakes!

What I realized was that while my son would benefit from the enrichment and socialization that preschool would bring, my main goal for preschool was meeting families in our neighborhood and finding more playmates for my extroverted son. We did lots of hands-on activities at home, so academic challenge wasn't that important at this stage of his life.

92

After reconsidering the options, I chose the parent cooperative preschool that met in a church basement in our neighborhood. Sure, the classroom was old-fashioned, but the involvement of the families (and very reasonable tuition) meant that we truly did become part of a community.

In retrospect, taking the time to think through all the aspects of what we were looking for in a preschool helped me make a better decision, and I avoided the nonsense of becoming a slave to tuition payments.

Carla, mom of two

MomSense from Other Mothers

What mommy issues do you find it difficult to keep in perspective?

The whole "this too shall pass" stuff, like potty-training or biting; it feels like it will never end when you're living through it. —Christine, mom of three

It's hard for me to watch my child go through life lessons, like not getting invited to a birthday party or losing his favorite toy, and keep it in perspective. I need to keep telling myself that these are just small things he needs to learn from and he will be just fine. —Jaime, mom of one

I always found it helpful to remind myself, and tell my children, that I am the BEST mother they've ever had! —Karen, mom of three

Lack of sleep. My kids want to "snuggle" every night to help them fall asleep and it drives me bonkers. Why can't they just go to sleep by themselves? Oh wait, there will be a day I miss that request . . . my internal conversation every night. –Alexandra, mom of three

Your MomSense

- Do you feel more judged or accepted by other moms?
- What matters most to you?
- Write three things that distract you from seeing the bigger picture:

Challenge: Find a mom who you think has different perspectives than you do and hang out with her a bit. Look for and enjoy the aspects in life that bond you together.

8

Sense of Self-Control

You have to decide what your highest priorities are and
have the courage . . . to say "no" to other things. And the
way to do that is by having a bigger "yes" burning inside.

Stephen Covey

When the two words chocolate and self-control collide in
my life, chocolate usually wins. I have little self-control when it comes to turning
down chocolate, chocolate chip cookies,
chocolate brownies, chocolate candy bars,
and especially Nutella. (Note: If you don't
know what Nutella is, it's a hazelnut fla-
vored chocolate spread that's amazing on anything. On our
recent backpacking trip we spread Nutella on everything.

> Me: chocolate +
> self-control =
> more chocolate.

One of the guys actually slathered it on a bagel and topped it off with cheddar cheese and a hunk of salami.)

If we have a jar of Nutella sitting around our house, I feel like it's a magnet for my hand and a spoon. It calls to me from the pantry. I lose my mind for a few moments, and the next thing I remember I'm washing off the spoon and hiding it in the dishwasher so no evidence exists that Mom was the one who had the last bite.

I keep buying it because it's a good excuse to practice self-control, and as a mom I've come to believe self-control is a necessary ingredient for successful parenting. Why? Because the ability to be in charge of your attitudes, actions, and behaviors is a critical life skill for adults and for children. And if we moms can model and encourage self-control, our children will adapt this trait in their own lives.

Ellen Galinsky, author of *Mind in the Making: The Seven Essential Life Skills Every Child Needs*, suggests self-control, or what she terms "inhibitory control," is one of the seven essential life skills. She defines this as the ability to refuse a strong desire to do one thing and instead do the most appropriate thing.

For example:

- Ignoring other distractions, such as the phone ringing or the dryer buzzing, and instead focusing on actively listening to the story your child is telling you.
- Refusing to buy Velcro shoes when teaching a child to tie her own shoes.
- Controlling the words you want to say when you're frustrated with your child for spilling his milk all over the kitchen table, and carefully choosing positive words instead.

- Deciding not to eat dessert because you want to lose weight even though everyone else around you is enjoying the yummy treat.
- Doing the commonplace tasks required in everyday life, such as putting groceries away, unloading the dishwasher, or playing Candy Land with your child, even when it's boring and you'd rather do something else.

Galinsky writes,

If we find it difficult sometimes to maintain our focus and self-control, imagine what it's like for our children, who don't have decades of practice and experience. These are difficult skills, which may be why they're so fundamentally important. On the other hand, these skills are like muscles—the more we work on them, the stronger they become. So there's always hope for our kids—and for us, too![1]

Mom Story

Time-Out for Mom

My fingers dug into my daughter's arms as I glared into her face. Her eyes opened wide. My intensity captured her full attention. Rage flooded my brain and I almost missed the small voice in my head warning me I was about to go over the edge. I stopped myself from throwing her onto the couch; instead I set her down roughly and stepped back.

"Mommy is taking a time-out." The words were forced out from my gritted teeth. "Do not move off this couch."

I will never forget the look on Maddy's face—the raw shock and fear.

I escaped to the safety of my bedroom and wept. I wept out of sadness that I had put my hands on my daughter in such anger. I wept for the fear in my little girl's eyes. But mostly I cried in tremendous relief.

What if I hadn't stopped when I did? There was a dark moment when I came close to losing control. And for a split second, I understood how a mom could possibly harm her own child. But I had been able to stop. Though the warning voice had been very quiet, I had heard it. And hearing it had brought a moment of clarity. A moment I had been working for and praying for when I realized I could not control my anger on my own. I did not want to be an out-of-control mother. I wanted to be a mom who wouldn't act out of blind rage—a mom who could control herself. And I had managed to do it. Not perfectly, but I had finally been able to hear my heart and be the mother I wanted to be in that awful moment.

After my tears were spent, I washed my face and braced myself. I had a four year old to apologize to.

My daughter was on the couch where I had left her. My tears sprang up anew as I knelt down.

"I am so sorry I lost my temper, sweetie. Are you okay?" She nodded. "I am sorry for scaring you. Will you forgive me?"

Chubby arms wrapped tight around my neck. "I love you, Momma!" Maddy squeezed tight. I squeezed back.

I will never forget what I realized that day: I can be more like the mom I see in my heart. Not a perfect mom, but a mom who can learn from experience and know God is helping me because he doesn't expect me to become the mom I want to be all on my own.

Melissa, mom of three

Every mom I know, if she's honest, has experienced a moment where she feels she lost her self-control and might even have had a thought about how she could have hurt her child. Continually practicing self-control, choosing to do the appropriate thing when we feel like doing something else, will become a natural part of our MomSense.

MomSense from Other Mothers

How do you practice self-control in your home?

We all go to our rooms if we feel like we are getting out of control-even Mommy. It has helped to refocus our attention and treat each other as we want to be treated. I tell my boys it is OK to be angry, but how you express your anger is the key to maturity and self-control. –Kim, mom of two

When I lose control, I always remember to acknowledge it to my kids, often with an apology for that, and remind them we are all human and fail at times. –Diana, mom of two

I think part of being so stressed is losing a part of ourselves in our kids. Whether you are a single parent or with a spouse, you should take time at least once a week to do what you want so that you can go home with a clear head. This takes down the stress level a little at a time. –Toni, mom of two

The power of self-control is at its optimum when you determine for yourself to never give up, and to own the moments that you do fall short so that you may learn from them quickly and keep forward momentum. –April, mom of three

Advantages of Teaching Children Self-Control

Because we live in such an instant society, self-control is not something children necessarily have to learn. Children today usually get what they want almost immediately. Encouraging self-control is something we have to intentionally instill in our children, and it is a skill that will bring them success and personal satisfaction in numerous ways as they grow up.

Ellen Galinsky also describes the famous Marshmallow Test, a 1960s experiment conducted by Walter Mischel at Stanford University, which has become a classic in determining children's ability to resist temptation and to delay gratification. In other words, they exercised self-control.

In this experiment, four year olds were each taken into a room with a one-way mirror so researchers could observe their behavior but the child couldn't see them. The researcher placed a plate with one marshmallow on one side and two on the other side in front of the child. Beside the child was a bell he or she could ring.

The goal of the experiment was to set up a situation in which the child made a choice. The researcher asked each child if he or she would like to have one marshmallow now or two later. Most children said they wanted two marshmallows.

The researcher then explained a game they wanted to play with the child. They told the child they were going to leave the room. If the child waited for the researcher to return before eating a marshmallow, then he or she got to have two. If the child decided not to wait, he or she could ring the bell and the researcher would come back right away, but then the child only got one marshmallow.

During the experiment some of the children were left for as long as fifteen minutes. The children employed all sorts of self-control tactics to keep from eating the marshmallows. Some turned their backs on the treats, some stuck out their tongues but didn't lick the marshmallows, some sang songs to distract themselves, and some shook their heads as if telling themselves "no."

Mischel noted that the children who were most successful at delaying gratification didn't focus on the marshmallows, but distracted themselves and shifted their attention to doing or looking at something else.

Now, here's something interesting. Years later Mischel followed up on the children who participated in the 1968 study. He found that the children who were able to wait longer for the marshmallows seemed to be doing better academically and personally. They had higher SAT scores, better ratings on their ability to pursue academic and other goals, less drug use, higher self-esteem and self-worth, and higher success in relationships.

Galinsky, who spent years collecting research for her book and interviewing researchers, says,

> Mischel believes that these executive function skills should be promoted and reinforced by families and schools because they enable children to become able to manage frustrations and distress in ways that don't derail them from pursuing the goals that are important to them. Remember: focus and self-control are always exercised in the service of pursuing an important personal goal.[2]

If you decide to try the marshmallow test in your own home, don't consider it a forecast of your child's fate. The more important point is to encourage parents to consistently try to train children in the art of self-control.

Be creative, keep lots of marshmallows on hand, have fun, allow mistakes, and never give up. Let's make an effort to practice self-control, making it a part of who we are as we grow in our MomSense.

Your MomSense

- On a scale of one to ten, with one being pathetic and ten being excellent, where would you rate your own self-control?

- List two areas in your life where you feel you have good self-control and two areas where you feel you need improvement:

- List one thing you can do today to increase your own self-control:

- List one thing you can do today to help your child practice self-control:

9

Sense of Calm

A healthy mind has an easy breath.

Unknown

Sheer. Chaos.

Those are two words to describe motherhood. Little people create chaos. That's just what they do. I'll never forget Josh's fourth birthday party. For some insane reason we decided to have a jumping party. Seriously, that was the theme of this party. We had a dozen four year olds jumping around the house and the yard. We made up all sorts of jumping games and gave them lots of sugar—because apparently we didn't have enough chaos. Crazy, I know. Plus, Jordan was a two year old waddling around trying to keep up with his brother, and I was seven months pregnant with Jake. Did I mention my friends decided they could also hang out during the party, and that included their other little ones? The combination of sugar, four year olds, adults not paying attention, and a pregnant woman did not mix well together.

I started to feel panicky as I looked around the room and saw all these little faces with purple frosting mustaches bobbing up and down, their wet, sticky fingers rubbing along the walls, the curtains, the couch pillows, and the doorknobs. One little boy walked past me and up the two stairs into our kitchen, then tripped and dropped his paper plate facedown. The cake, frosting, and melted ice cream splattered on the floor. In his other hand he tried to balance a cup of juice, but as he wobbled the juice spilled over the edge of the cup and mixed with the mess on the floor.

Of course, I was the only one who noticed. I wanted to scream. Instead, I turned around and disappeared into the nearest bathroom and told myself to breathe. I was like one of our birthday party balloons, tight and full of air. Letting that air out of my lungs decreased the pressure and gave me some relief. I took several deep breaths and felt my heart slow down, my breathing slow down, and my mind slow down. That simple act helped me release some of my stress in my chaotic moment.

Breathing in and out does that for human beings. Everything about breathing is just miraculous. Breath gives us life. I've noticed when I feel scared, worried, anxious, or any other negative emotions, my breathing is erratic. But when I have a sense of peace I breathe calmly. So the first moment I feel anxious, stressed-out, or panicked, I stop and breathe.

Once I calm myself down, I can begin to take the next steps I need to keep that sense of peace whenever I feel like I'm losing it.

MomSense from Other Mothers

What do you do to calm yourself down?

Pack and go! When I feel that internal chaos I know I need to call a friend and go do something with someone else. —Nichole, mom of one

I give myself a couch day. It's sort of like a mental health day. I give myself mental permission to slow down and do nothing. —Jacque, mom of two

I like to take a bath. Something about running water helps my mind go blank and I can relax. —Michelle, mom of two

I go to the gym. —Elizabeth, mom of three

When I feel totally stressed I close my eyes and imagine myself as a wet rag being wrung out by giant hands, and I feel the stress dripping off my body like streams of water falling from the towel. This might sound weird, but visualizing this helps me feel a sense of peace. —Marie, mom of three

Many moms I've talked to think of peace as non-squabbling children; a calm, quiet, tranquil moment; or a day without any stress. That is a nice thought, but rare in the world of mom. Most days are filled with nursing babies, diapers, drives to and from preschool, lost favorite toys, meltdowns in the mall, projects at work, car breakdowns, walks with the dog, crickets for the gecko, and other forms of chaos. A mom's world is probably not going to become tranquil. The kind of peace I'm talking about is an inner peace in the midst of the chaos.

The other day I was watching a nest tucked under the eaves of our porch with several baby birds in it. Their little heads poked up over the edge of the nest and the mommy bird snuggled up next to them. Outside an intense Colorado spring thunderstorm was raging. The sky was steel gray, and sheets of rain poured from the sky before turning to golf ball sized hail. Deafening thunder shook our house and lightning erratically lit up the sky. I was amazed as I observed the mommy bird. She sat calmly in the nest with her babies. She wasn't freaking out like my yellow lab, Mogul, who was alternating between barking and cowering under the kitchen table because he's terrified of thunder. She exemplified the peace I want to have as a mom. An inner peace, a tranquil spirit—no matter what storms are raging around me.

Mom Story

Would Everyone Please Calm Down?

One of my favorite films is the story of a dad who strives for a "perfect" family celebration. Instead, everything goes wrong: unexpected guests arrive, the house gets destroyed, and any hopes for a meaningful experience lie in tatters. Predictably, the dad blows up in front of his whole family. He scoffs at the idea that things could get any worse, claiming they have already arrived at the threshold of hell.

I erupt into from-the-gut guffaws every time I see this scene. And it replays in my head when I have moments where I'm about to lose it, when I'm trying to make dinner with two screaming two year olds clinging to my legs, and two older children fighting in the next room.

With four children ages six, three, two, and two, my life rarely reflects a peaceful scene. Intentions of calm exchanges go up in puffs of smoke with the first, "Mama! Ella called me a poopy!" At times I can't even hear myself think amidst the four little voices clamoring for my attention. For a woman who craves alone time and prefers quiet, intimate gatherings to crowded, boisterous ones, learning to adjust to motherhood has been difficult. The chaos can be so overwhelming, and yet, I deeply desire to handle it with grace and wisdom. How do I stay calm when all I feel like doing is screaming?

Here's what I've come up with so far: The classical music station can work wonders in a car of cranky people. Getting outside for a walk or a visit to a playground burns energy like you wouldn't believe. Breathing deeply and then speaking softly often carries me through an onslaught of requests. And a daily dose of quiet time soothes not only little bodies, but mine too.

Not exactly rocket science, but it's a start. Of course, I still yell and stomp my feet and blow up in front of my whole family in ways I never thought I would. But my threshold for handling chaos continues to expand and my ability to respond gracefully increases. Every time I choose soft words over shouting, patience over irritability, or hugging over intolerance I claim a small victory.

Tally, mom of four

So, how does a mom learn to grow her sense of peace?

Breathe. As Tally suggested in her story, stop and breathe before saying or doing anything. Once we calm ourselves down, we can take positive next steps.

Prioritize. Most of us live a fast-paced, frantic life. One almost sure way to increase calm in a home is to cut out some of the chaos. We set ourselves up for panic attacks as we register our darling children for soccer, baseball, piano, pottery, swim lessons, Spanish lessons, play dates, and so on. Our desire to raise our progenies with all sorts of excellent skills has taken a toll on the family. I won't stay on my soapbox too long, but I really believe we've become dysfunctional as a society with our tendency to over-schedule our children. We desire to give them good experiences—and that should include running around the neighborhood playing "kick the can," getting all the way to "Mom, I'm bored," and looking for bugs in the backyard. Stop the madness. Slow down. Let kids be kids.

Choose what you want to do. You don't have to do it all. I have a friend who reminded me of the time her cat became sick and she had to take the animal to the veterinarian. She was eight months pregnant and also had a three year old toddling along. The vet examined the cat and didn't find anything really wrong, but did notice the cat's teeth weren't looking so good. So, she proceeded to instruct my friend on how to brush her cat's teeth. My disheveled friend stood there with her bulging belly, a toddler clinging to her leg, and a sick cat in her arms. She looked at the vet, ready to scream or slap her in the face, but instead she gritted her teeth and said, "Look at me. Do you think I'm going to take the time to brush my cat's teeth?" The vet, humbled, acknowledged the truth. "No, you're right. Don't worry about it. The cat will be fine."

Seriously? People brush their cat's teeth? We really don't have to do it all.

Stop and breathe. Prioritize. Then try to pray and trust.

Pray. When I don't know what to do, I do what I know I can do—and I can always pray. Prayer is part of the process of growing in peace. When I pray, I communicate with God about my heart, my stresses, and my circumstances, and that often brings me a sense of peace. Prayer can happen anytime, anywhere. No matter what is going on around me I know God can hear me. Sometimes I have those sweet, quiet prayer times before everyone wakes up, other times I just send a simple sentence up to God, and sometimes only one word—like "help!"

Trust. I love to scuba dive. But when I first learned, it was terrifying. The idea of submerging myself forty to a hundred feet underwater and breathing into the regulator seemed insane. I had to force myself, against all that seemed logical, to let the air out of my vest, submerge myself completely, and breathe. My heart pounded. My breaths were shallow and fast. But the equipment worked. After a few minutes I stopped panicking and took deep, slow gulps of oxygen. The air from my tank filled my lungs. I was breathing underwater. Amazing! I had to trust my equipment more than my scared mind, which was telling me, "This is impossible." I could hear myself breathing in and out. Everything else was silent. I looked around me and saw the most amazing fish, coral, and seashells. Before long I experienced a sense of peace.

Learning to trust in God is a little like scuba diving. I've had to release my fears into much bigger hands. When I do this as a mom, I discover a peace like no other.

Sometimes the chaos is within us. We battle our own desires and if-onlys. Motherhood is beautiful, but sometimes it doesn't look like we thought it would. When chaos reigns inside of us, it's time to work on trust. Once we make personal, needed changes or find a place of acceptance and internal peace, then we will experience less chaos—or at least become better able to manage the normal chaos of motherhood.

Breathe. Prioritize. Pray. Trust. Sounds simple, doesn't it? But sometimes it feels impossible. It's a good thing God promises to help. Jesus, before leaving his disciples, said, "Peace I leave with you; my peace I give to you. I do not give to you as the world gives. Do not let your hearts be troubled and do not be afraid" (John 14:27).

When the stresses of each day smother those feelings of peace, you'll find peace is more than just a feeling. It's an inner tranquil spirit a mom can have in the midst of sheer chaos.

Your MomSense

- What do you do to calm yourself down?
- What does a "sense of peace" mean to you?
- Describe a recent time you experienced a lack of peace, and what you could have done differently to find peace in that moment:

_____

_____

_____

- Plan ahead for chaos. What is your personal plan to practice growing your sense of inner peace?

10

Sense of Joy

If you can't make it better, you can laugh at it.

Erma Bombeck

Quiz

The last time I laughed was: _____

The funniest movie I've ever seen is: _____

Someone with a good sense of humor is someone who:

_____

I think God created us to have a sense of humor because:

_____

When my child dumps the flour all over the kitchen floor, steps in it, and then makes footprints and handprints throughout the house, I:

a) scream;

b) put him into time-out and clean up the mess;

c) grab my camera, take a picture, and post it on Facebook immediately; or

d) take off my shoes and join the fun.

"I have a sense of humor."

_____ True, and here's why:

_____

_____

_____

_____ I used to, before I had kids. (Read on to rediscover your sense of humor.)

_____ False (But you want to find it, right?)

One day I was wandering around a bookstore, killing time before picking up my kids from school, when my cell phone rang. I dug it out of my purse and answered it.

"Ms. Blackmer?" a woman's voice asked.

"Yes," I replied.

"This is Ms. Fernandez, the vice principal for Manhattan School. I'm calling because Jake was involved in an incident and I wanted to discuss it with you. He's okay; I just want to tell you what happened so when he gets home from school today you'll be able to talk with him about it."

"Oh, okay. . . . What happened?" I felt fearful because I had no idea what she was about to tell me. *But Jake's a good kid*, I reassured myself. *He's not one to get into trouble— he just won the Rotary good citizenship award for middle school students, remember?* But as a mom, I'd learned you just never know and you need to be prepared to deal with whatever. I took a deep breath and braced myself for what I was about to hear.

Ms. Fernandez then proceeded to tell me the story.

That morning Jake had ridden the bus to school wearing a jacket he hadn't worn for several months. In the jacket pocket was a box he had found on an adventure in the mountains with Zane, his brothers, another dad, and his two boys. That day, Jake discovered a cool looking box with a wolf on the top. Instead of throwing it away, he stuck it in his pocket to bring home and put on his shelf. He's a "collector" type kid. He's always collected rocks, sticks, deer antlers, coins, seashells, and all sorts of stuff and displayed them in his room. Well, he promptly forgot about the box, and it sat in his coat pocket for months.

This particular day was chilly, so Jake grabbed the jacket with the box in its pocket and jumped on the bus. At some point, the box fell out of Jake's pocket and onto the bus floor. Jake had no idea he'd lost the box.

Once the bus driver had all the kids off the bus and returned to the bus terminal he did his normal walk through—looking for forgotten jackets, hats, gloves, lunch boxes, the usual. This time he found an empty box—and it turned out he was familiar with guns and knew instantly this was an ammunition box. He did what any responsible bus driver should do if he finds an empty bullet box on his bus: he called the police.

The police called the schools, which went immediately into lockdown. Then the police and their K9 dogs descended on the schools. They searched every locker, which took a couple of hours. Because they didn't find anything, they asked for all the kids on that bus to come to the library. One by one, they were asked to meet alone with two officers and a German shepherd. First the officers frisked them, while the dog sniffed around, and then they were interrogated. It was intimidating for all the kids, not to mention they were all very hungry. This took place over the lunch hour, and no one was allowed to go to lunch until this was figured out. When they questioned Jake, they asked if he'd seen any kind of box on the bus that morning. At first he said no. Then a light bulb went on in his head. "Oh yeah! There was a box in my coat pocket. I forgot."

"What did the box look like?" one of the officers asked.

"It had a wolf on the top . . ." Jake went on to describe the box. It was obvious to them that Jake meant no harm, and it was all a big accident. They told Jake they understood he didn't even know he had an ammunition box and that he wasn't in any kind of trouble. The mystery was solved. The school resumed its schedule, kids went to a very late lunch, and everyone went home on the bus like every other day. And that was it.

When Jake came home I could tell he was shaken up. It was a scary day for everyone, and he knew he had unintentionally caused it. He told Josh, Jordan, and me what had happened.

"Sick!" (in a good way) the boys yelled as they gave Jake a high-five, helping Jake feel a tad better.

Then we called Zane, who was out of town. I watched Jake retell the story to his dad and then watched him smile and start laughing. I could tell he felt relief; the laughter did him good.

"What was so funny?" I asked when he hung up the phone.

"When I told Dad that both schools were closed for a few hours, he said, 'Jake, I tried my whole life to close down my schools when I was a kid, and you did it without even trying; that's not fair.'"

This totally cracked Jake up and seemed to help him with the bad feelings he was having about the whole incident.

I wish we didn't live in a time when we have to worry about our kids' safety at school, but we do. But knowing our son and his sincere mistake, I think our joking about it at home helped him to recover from the strain of the day. He was then able to laugh at himself and the situation he had inadvertently caused.

Benefits of Laughter

Physical	Mental	Social
• Boosts immunity	• Adds joy to life	• Strengthens relationships
• Lowers stress hormones	• Decreases anxiety	• Attracts others to you
• Decreases pain	• Decreases fear	• Increases teamwork
• Relaxes muscles	• Relieves stress	• Helps defuse conflict
• Prevents heart disease	• Improves mood	• Promotes bonding[1]
	• Enhances resilience	

We could have gone down several different roads in reacting to this situation. We could have become upset, making Jake more upset. We could have lectured Jake on checking his pockets, blaming him and making him feel really bad—or we could find the humor in it. We could acknowledge it was a silly mistake and take the pressure off of him. Once we started joking around, I could see a physical difference in Jake's demeanor. He was smiling and seemed much more lighthearted.

A sense of humor is an essential element in a mom's Mom-Sense. Knowing when to laugh and lighten a moment can have an amazing effect on any situation. Did you know a sense of humor is emotionally, physically, and socially good for you? If you model a sense of humor to your children, they will also reap the emotional and physical benefits of laughter.

Mom Story

Kids Say the Funniest Things

I slowly lowered my hips into the driver's seat, my bulging belly rubbing the steering wheel. At eight months pregnant, I was tired. The last thing I wanted to do was get out of the house. But when a friend from high school offered hand-me-down infant clothes, I eagerly surrendered my daily nap to meet her.

Carol opened the door. "Oh, Joyce, it's great to see you," she said with a giggle as she tried hugging my shoulders. "Come in."

Walking through the foyer, I noticed three-year-old Michelle hiding behind her mother.

"Hi, honey," I called, looking her way.

Michelle clutched her mommy's legs tighter.

I sat down on the couch. As Carol made me a glass of iced tea, I fingered the tiny washcloths, onesies, and blankets piled in a box. "Oh, Carol, these are great. Thank you so much."

My friend sat on the other end of the couch. Pulling Michelle on her lap, my friend explained that she was giving me the baby items she used a few years ago when Michelle was an infant.

"You're a big girl now, and you don't need these things," she explained to her daughter. "We're giving Miss Joyce your clothes to use for her new baby."

Just then, I felt my baby kick.

"Oh, Michelle," I said, putting my hand on my tummy. "The baby just kicked; do you want to see if you can feel the baby?"

Michelle extended her tiny arm and put her hand on my belly. Then Michelle turned her face toward mine, brown eyes curious. She asked, in a serious tone, "Why did you eat your baby?"

Joyce, mom of two

Families who laugh and play together enjoy being together, and who doesn't want that? As moms, we can be instigators of laughter in our homes. For some moms this is easy. For others, especially those of us who are working on discovering and growing our sense of humor, this might take more practice. If you want to increase the humor in your own life and in your home, here are some things to try:

- smile
- count your blessings
- when you hear laughter move toward it
- spend time with playful people
- ask others to tell you something funny from their day
- watch funny movies
- watch funny YouTube videos
- go to a family-friendly comedy show
- read comic books
- visit the humor section in your local bookstore
- laugh at yourself
- tell most embarrassing moments
- tell your children funny things they did when they were little
- play with a puppy
- eat ice cream often
- watch the monkeys at the zoo
- watch a preschooler

Growing a sense of humor is just the beginning of creating something vital in our homes—an atmosphere of joy.

Atmosphere is defined as "the dominant mood or emotional tone." What is the dominant mood or emotional tone of your home? Creating a foundation of joy will help us and our children answer this question in a positive light. To describe their home as a happy place is something most women long for. In *What Women Want: The Life You Crave and How God Satisfies*, Lisa T. Bergren and Rebecca Price quote a survey: "Whether married or single, divorced or widowed, younger or older, the desire for a happy home life topped nearly everyone's list of wants, needs and priorities."[2]

I'm going to challenge us to take this emotion deeper and create an underlying foundation to build our homes upon—to experience joy no matter what our circumstances. Joy is more than a happy feeling and more than having fun. Joy is a deep sense of contentment, acceptance, and hope—an unwavering source to base your home life upon.

Elisa Morgan describes the difference between joy and happiness in her book *Naked Fruit: Getting Honest about the Fruit of the Spirit.* She explains that happiness is circumstantial, a feeling you have when whatever happens makes you feel good. Then she writes,

> Joy is a confidence in God no matter what *happens.* Because we've watched God working in so many moments of life— good, bad, confusing, sorrowful, challenging, unfathomable—when we are joyful we are wrapped up by our observations and held in place, knowing clearly that just as God came through before, he will come through again.[3]

Underneath every blooming flower is an intricate root system holding the flower in place and nourishing it. This is what an atmosphere of joy can be to a family. When circumstances arise that are not funny, and do not make you feel happy, what are you going to do? There has to be something more substantial to hold on to than just feeling happy, especially for the millions of women (and men) who suffer from depression.

Mom Story

Hope in Her Darkest Days

After the birth of each of my children, I suffered severe bouts of depression. Then life really came crashing down on my thirtieth birthday. I was at church with my two preschool age children; we were in the crowded parking lot in the rain, and I thought, *Why are all these people smiling?* I was overcome with sadness for no explainable reason. I went home, curled up on my bed, pulled the sheets

over my head, and entered my cocoon. Before long
my only goal was to get out of bed and dressed each
day. Some days I couldn't even do that.

Depression is lonely. I couldn't be around
people because they were happy and I was not. I
turned down social invitations, or just didn't show
up. Soon, everybody just quit calling, quit invit-
ing. After awhile we didn't have any friends, and
friends were what we needed.

Work was impossible. How many times can you
call your boss and say, "Hey, I can't make it in
today, I'm sad." I stopped going to church, stopped
going to my kids' school programs and games, and
shut down even further.

Jim, my husband, went into function mode; he
had to be both mother and father to the kids. This
just made me feel even guiltier. I wasn't the person, wife, mom, friend I wanted to be. I began to
think I was ruining everyone's life. I wanted to
die. I thought about it all the time. All the time.

One Wednesday afternoon I hit rock bottom. Jim
came home to find me wedged between the bed and the
wall in hysterics, begging God to let me die. I was
hospitalized and began intense treatment for my
depression. The next several years were a rollercoaster of emotions. Some days were good, some bad.
Sometimes I was energetic and happy, other days I
cried, and some days I was angry. I was especially
angry with God. I had done everything I was sup-
posed to do but still battled depression. *God,
where are you?* I wondered.

Then came the day I was home alone all day, exhausted and very angry. I began to pray out loud
until I didn't have any more words to tell God my
pain. I laid down on the couch and I prayed, "Somebody has got to pray for me. I can't do it anymore.

I don't even know what to pray for." At that moment I felt a comforting presence. I knew it was Jesus wrapping his arms around me, and I knew he was praying for me. I could feel it. I felt joy—not happiness, but joy—for the first time in a long time.

I wish I could wrap up my story with a nice pretty bow and say I've never had to fight depression again, but that's not true. I fight depression every day, but I'm reminded that even when I run out of words to pray Jesus prays for me. I know he is always with me. He is my strength when mine is gone. Having this hope gives me joy even in my darkest days.

Robin, mom of two

Believe Robin. It is possible for a deep sense of joy to remain even in the midst of depression or darkness.

MomSense from Other Mothers

What's the greatest joy you've discovered through mothering?

LOVE . . . it is amazing to see and feel so much love! –Jessica, mom of three

How stinking funny my kids are. –Katherine, mom of two

Watching my children learn new things. –Kendra, mom of three

Just the joy of seeing life through a child's eyes. –Susan, mom of three

Even in the midst of challenges we can still experience joy. Recently I was in an exercise class, and during the most difficult exercise (imagine your gluteus maximus muscles aching as you balance on your hands and knees doing what's called the fire hydrant . . . okay, maybe you *don't* want to imagine that) the instructor says, "Find the joy even in this."

Everyone in the class groaned and some laughed, but then she reminded us that the pain was doing our bodies good. It did make me feel a little joy inside; I knew I would experience good benefits for putting my body through this agony. I didn't enjoy it at the moment and I can't say I was feeling happy, but I did have hope I was getting healthier and would eventually see the rewards of this exercise. This is sort of what joy is like in life. When you exercise your joy in good times, you'll be able to experience that same sense of joy in the challenging times. Just hold on to the hope that you are growing, no matter what your circumstances, into the woman God wants you to be.

Developing your sense of humor and creating a foundation for joy will give depth to your MomSense, and will ultimately help you create a healthy, joyful atmosphere in your home for you and your family.

Your MomSense

- I would describe the difference between happiness and joy as:

- List three things you can do to create a more joyful atmosphere in your family life:

  _____

  _____

  _____

- If you could do something to add joy to someone else's life today, what would you do? (Now go and do it!)

11

Sense of Love

The supreme happiness of life is the conviction that we are loved.

Victor Hugo

When we build a family, the foundation we build upon is crucial. Our foundation will become the strength of our families both in the pleasant times and when the storms hit. The essential element that inhabits all of our MomSense is love. I know that sounds obvious, but we often overlook the obvious. MomSense and love go hand in hand. Becoming a mom opens up a whole new world of what it means to really love another person differently than we've ever loved before.

Most of us have probably experienced romantic love, or at least watched it play out on a big screen before our eyes. It's wonderful and mysterious, amazing and miraculous. It's an adventure and something I hope everyone experiences in life. But I experienced a different kind of love when I first held my baby in my arms, looked into his eyes, touched his toes, kissed his forehead, and felt his warm breath on my chin as he slept on my chest.

Loving a child is such a profound feeling that it's almost impossible to put into words. Yet we use the word we have—love. This is the same word we use to say we love a pair of shoes or we love chocolate, but that kind of expression doesn't even begin to compare with what it means to say "I love my child."

In ancient Greek there are three different words for our one English word, "love," and each of these three words carries a very different meaning.

Eros: romantic, passionate love.

Philia: friendship-type love.

Agape: the highest form of love—an unconditional love for others despite their flaws and weaknesses. This is the word used in the Bible to describe God's love for humanity.

Agape love is what I aim for when creating a parenting philosophy for my family. This is the type of love I see in families I admire. Fully knowing and still fully loving another human being is the best definition of unconditional love I can think of. *Agape* means totally accepting another person—body, mind, and spirit—and having a willingness to make personal sacrifices to exhibit love for someone else. Agape love is:

• patient	• faithful	• trusting
• kind	• accepting	• self-sacrificing
• forgiving	• hopeful	• believing

- protecting
- enduring
- absolute

- merciful
- unselfish
- confident

- optimistic

Agape love is not:

- impatient
- unkind
- deceitful
- hurtful
- unfaithful

- jealous
- proud
- rude
- selfish
- negative

- tiring
- overbearing
- controlling
- demanding
- fearful

It's easier to love our children unconditionally when they are newborns. Nothing compares to that experience. And thank God he lets us experience that type of love for our babies—so when they're toddlers throwing a temper tantrum at the park, we remember how much we love them, even though we might not feel it right at that moment. Or when they're teenagers and really testing our love, our mother love and our "loving" responses are ingrained in our memories and help us through the trying times.

Mother Love

Mother love is a fierce love. It's an intense love. Mothers are overwhelmed, obsessed, and completely crazy with love for their children, whether natural born or adopted. Every mom I know would throw herself in front of a bus if it meant saving her child. She would protect her babies with a vicious determination to let no one or no thing bring them harm. Never mess with a mama.

So, if this mother love is so natural and powerful, then why do moms need to develop it as a parenting foundation? Because we forget.

As time passes, we forget those days of snuggling with our baby. We forget the smell of the lotion we slather on their bodies. And we don't always feel love. Sometimes love becomes a choice. We choose to love even when we don't feel like it, and this choice will be easier if we practice loving intentionally.

Intentionally creating a home built on unconditional love will help create a loving environment for a lifetime. When we face turbulent times and storms that threaten to harm our families, the love we built our families upon will be the glue that will hold us together—no matter what.

And during the pleasant times, a family who learns to love unconditionally will enjoy the rewards of finding this type of relationship with each other. A home filled with unconditional love will create sweet memories for all who experience it.

MomSense from Other Mothers

Definitions of unconditional love:

Love no matter what, under all circumstances. —Julie, mom of two

To me it means loving all of them—the good, the bad, and the ugly. It also means never giving up on them, no matter how hard it might get. —Christine, mom of four

Loving them when you're not liking them! —Shelley, mom of three

When you love someone unconditionally you do not put limits on that love. Certain circumstances would not cause you to keep from loving them, and nothing would cause you to stop loving that person. —Terry, mom of three

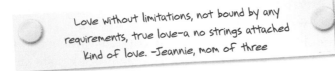

Love without limitations, not bound by any requirements, true love–a no strings attached kind of love. –Jeannie, mom of three

This is what we all long for, and as moms we can give this to our children. Part of our MomSense is this love we live and feel for our children, naturally and innately. But sometimes love and other emotions get tangled. Instead of something we freely give, it becomes something to be earned. As her children grow up, a mom's love can become very performance oriented. Her child feels loved when he does well, but if he makes any mistakes he senses disappointment and a lack of love.

Alternately, some women become "smother lovers." We mean well, but you could say some moms just love too much. We smother our children to the point where they become so dependent on us they are incapable of finding love and life on their own.

It's healthy to think about what kind of love we want to give, and what we don't want our love to grow into.

Fearless Love

A newfound fear emerged in me when I became a mom. Handling my little baby was scary. I felt terrified to give him his first bath, afraid his soapy little body would slip out of my hands, and his head would go underwater even for a moment and cause him to be forever afraid of water. I was scared to put him in and take him out of his car seat—what if I accidentally bonked the tender spot on his head with the seat buckle? I was afraid he might stop breathing at night. At times I would sleep on the floor next to his crib. The fears

I discovered in my new mom world were too numerous to name. I was a walking, sleepy, scared woman.

It took time for me to become confident in my ability to take care of my children. I did accidentally bonk them once or twice on the head, and they were okay. I started to recognize when my imagination was ruling my logical thought life and taking my mind down a path of fearful thoughts. I learned to intentionally stop my thoughts, calm down, and talk sense to myself. I didn't want to be a fearful mom, always worrying about what might happen. I wanted to be a fearless and wise woman. *Be sensible, not fearful* is what I told myself—and still do. I want to live with boldness, confident about my life and my mothering rather than apprehensive.

Often fear is a protective instinct. It is part of our Mom-Sense. Listening to our fears and shielding our kids from harm is part of what we do. But, as I know from experience, loving from a fearful place is not good for anyone. Fear, which can become irrational, actually causes a physical response in your body. Fear triggers anxiety, worry, fright, paranoia, horror, and dread. If we're fearful moms we will raise fearful, timid children. We all know a mom like that. She won't let her children do anything even remotely dangerous, and her child is afraid of his own shadow. This fearful type of love does not encourage confident, independent children.

Mom Story
Fear = More Anxiety

I was lying in my tent on top of my sleeping bag, reading a book. I had my head resting on a pillow and was relishing a few moments of peace during a lazy afternoon on our family camping trip. Out of the blue I heard a crash, and then my whole body jerked. I remember the book flying out of my hands and through the air. I tried to call out to my husband, Doug, and that's all I remember.

I woke up in the hospital later, my mom holding my hand and my friend Katie standing next to my bed. Turns out, the tree next to my tent, whose root system I was lying on top of, was struck by lightning. The electric current flowed through the roots, up through my sleeping bag, and then through my body. I had burns from the zipper of my shorts and the underwire of my bra and extensive nerve damage, but I was alive.

The first question out of my mouth was, "Are my ovaries okay?" I wanted desperately to have children. Yes, my ovaries were fine. Then I said to my friend, "This has been a lousy day." Then I went back to sleep.

My recovery was long and painful. Adding to the physical issues, I also suffered from Post Traumatic Stress Disorder (PTSD). I experienced extreme anxiety, loss of appetite, and loss of sleep. I couldn't function normally. I went to counseling, took medication, and did acupuncture to help me through it.

A couple of years later I became pregnant and had my first child, Isaac. My pregnancy and birth experience created the perfect storm that reignited my PTSD. As a new mommy, I started experiencing extreme panic attacks. Again, normal functioning became impossible. I feared I was going crazy. The enormity of my responsibility of taking care of my son terrified me. I operated with this overwhelming sense of fear, and it was not healthy for my husband, my son, or me.

I knew I was not okay, and Doug encouraged me to get whatever help I needed. I went to the hospital at my lowest point. Then I started getting counseling again, took anti-anxiety medication, and relied on Doug and my friends when I needed help.

I'm doing well now and can see how this experience makes me a healthier, stronger mom. I learned mothering from a place of fear only leads to more anxiety. I've slowly learned to let go of my control and fears, and ultimately I've learned to trust God more in my life and my family's lives.

Nikki, mom of one

As Nikki expresses in her story, fear is a sister to control. When fear raises its ugly head it is usually in association with feeling out of control. Not being in control is scary. But the truth is we are not in control as much as we like to think we are. One of the first steps in the twelve-step recovery program is acknowledging a higher power. Freedom from fear is discovered when one lets go of control. Growing in our conviction that there is a God and trusting that he is ultimately the one in control takes a heavy burden off our backs. One of my favorite Bible verses about this is: "There is no fear in love. But perfect love drives out fear" (1 John 4:18).

Fear-based mothering, such as making decisions because we are afraid for our children or of the world they live in, leads to more anxiety and often produces anxious children. If we can mother from a place of fearless love by letting go of our control and trusting in God more than ourselves, we will be taking a giant step in the direction of loving unconditionally, not restrained or paralyzed from a sense of fear.

Boundless Love

"Boundless" means loving people without expectations or requirements, and letting go of expecting anything in return.

We love our children and they will love us back as best they can, but there will be times when we won't get any kudos from anyone. We'll fix thousands of meals, do mountains of laundry, and pick up truckloads of toys—and rarely receive a big hug or a "thank you" for what we do.

Boundless love is others-oriented. It's denying our own needs for the benefit of someone else. Loving sacrificially is definitely part of our MomSense DNA. From day one, whether a woman gives birth or adopts, that child's needs come first. We give up sleep to feed them throughout the night. We give up our right to eat when we want because our babies need to eat first. And as anyone who's gone through pregnancy knows, we give up control over our own bodies. We morph into something completely beautiful and bizarre (more bizarre than beautiful for me, anyway), and the living being inside of us takes what he or she needs to grow. Putting others' needs before our own becomes a way of life for almost every mom. As she grows in her life and love for her children, she often gives up her own needs to meet those of others. This loving without expectations or demands from others signifies a mom who is maturing in her love, learning to love with a pure heart, and loving unconditionally.

Loving Ourselves

As we live sacrificially and give so much of ourselves to our families, we still need to take loving care of ourselves. If a mom becomes too empty from giving to others, she will have nothing more to give. In *How Full Is Your Bucket? Positive Strategies for Work and Life*, authors Tom Rath and Donald O. Clifton write, "Each of us has an invisible bucket, it is constantly emptied or filled depending on what others say or do to us. When our bucket is full we feel great. When it's empty we feel awful."[1]

Although this book primarily addresses interpersonal relationships, I think the concept can be taken to an individual level. We cannot totally rely on others to fill our buckets, but must find ways to help ourselves fill our own buckets. Maybe for you it's going for a bike ride, seeing a movie, spending some alone time in a quiet place, reading a novel, or taking a bubble bath. Just keep doing those little things that help you feel full as a woman, and then you'll be a better mom.

As always, figuring out how to balance our needs with the needs of others can be tricky, especially for moms. At times we aren't able to meet our needs, such as when a child is so sick we have to cancel everything on our to-do list to take care of her. But that doesn't mean we should never do anything for ourselves. Moms, let's not let our internal buckets run dry. When we keep doing things that feed our souls, we will have so much more to give.

A special bond is created between a mom and her child. We see it over and over again. We see big tough football players break down in tears when they thank their moms. We see husky bikers with heart tattoos on their bulging biceps with "mom" written in the middle. (I was so happy when my son came home with that drawn on his cast.) Even Sandra Bullock in her Oscar acceptance speech for best actress in the movie *Blind Side* gave credit to moms everywhere for the incredible roles they play in real life.

A mother's love is the beginning of a lifetime of love for her little ones. A mother sets the stage for the future and affects the love her children will give and receive the rest of their lives. God has given us the responsibility of mothering, and he's also provided us with what we need to give love to those around us—our astounding sense of love that's a part of our

MomSense. The type of love a child experiences at home will ultimately affect how he or she perceives, gives, and receives love—and how he or she will view God and God's love.

Your MomSense

- What are some of your greatest fears as a mom? Share these with other moms.
- How can you become more confident in your MomSense and let go of your fears?
- What expectations are you holding on to that you might need to let go?
- Describe your sense of balance between loving sacrificially and meeting your own needs:

- How can you practice loving your family unconditionally?

12

Mama Dramas

Here's a chance to put your MomSense into practice. Below are several mothering dilemmas based on issues from real moms just like you. Remember, there is no one "right" answer. These are suggested solutions based on research, personal experience, and real mom advice.[1] Have fun exploring these and other issues, and discover strategies to handle various parenting dilemmas.

Mama Drama One: Biting

Your two-year-old son just bit his best friend's hand. What should you do?

1. Address your son immediately, telling him biting is not allowed;

2. Leave the room because you're so frustrated with your son;
3. Give your attention to the child who was bitten, saying something like, "Ouch, that must hurt. Let's go put some ice on it.";
4. Ask your still-angry child, "Why did you bite your friend?"; or
5. Encourage the other child to bite your son back so he can see how it feels.

Suggested Solutions

The best immediate response is to let your son know that biting is not allowed and then give comforting attention to the child who was bitten. It is not a good idea to ask your angry child why he bit his friend, because a still-furious child will most likely not be able to articulate his reasons. Biting is a common behavior for two and three year olds. A young child who bites occasionally is going through a normal developmental stage and is not destined to become a bully.

Mama Drama Two: Temper Tantrum

Your eighteen-month-old daughter throws a fit in the grocery store because you won't buy her the cupcakes with the pretty pink icing covered with sparkly green sugar. What should you do?

1. Ignore the tantrum;
2. Buy the cupcakes so she'll stop screaming and deal with it when you get home;
3. Sit down on the floor and throw your own fit;
4. Ask a supermarket employee to watch your grocery cart while you take your daughter out to the car to calm down; or

5. Use the "art of distraction" to draw her attention to something silly or funny or interesting.

Suggested Solutions

If ignoring the tantrum works, then that's a good place to start. If not, then try the distraction technique. If that doesn't work, it's okay to ask someone else for help. It's no big deal to leave your cart and come back when your child is calm. My guess is the other shoppers and employees will respect you for it. And if you do give in and buy the cupcakes, even if you feel like you shouldn't, you won't be the first mom to cave. Don't sweat it. The next time you may be better able to deal with a tantrum. One of the most important things to remember is to keep calm. No matter what, don't throw a tantrum of your own.

Mama Drama Three: Sibling Squabbling

You enter the playroom to find your two boys slugging each other because they both wanted to play with the same toy truck—and this is the fifth fight they've had today. What are some ways to squelch this constant sibling squabbling?

1. Sit back and watch them battle it out;
2. Separate your kids immediately and allow them to play alone in their own space for a while;
3. Offer some possible solutions such as setting a timer with an equal amount of time for each child to play with the truck; or
4. Throw the truck in the trash can so they can't fight about it anymore.

Suggested Solutions

Sibling rivalry is a mom issue that's been around since the beginning of time. It's one of those issues that can make the most calm, sane mom lose her mind—and it's good to remind yourself it is normal behavior. All families deal with it.

First, it's important to set some very specific ground rules for your family, such as no punching, biting, kicking, or name-calling. When your children get into a physical tussle, they need to be separated immediately and reminded of those firm rules. Have some age-appropriate consequence ready for breaking those rules. If you can't think of an appropriate consequence, it's fine to say, "Mommy needs some time to think about what to do about this."

Separating squabbling siblings is also a good idea; they may just need some time away from each other. If a battle has not turned into a wrestling match it's okay to let them try to work things out on their own. You won't always be around to settle their differences, and learning to negotiate disagreements with others is an important, lifelong skill. Throwing away the toy is one way to avoid another fight about it, but a better option is to give your children tools to learn how to share.

Calling in help if you're about to lose it might be just what you need. But don't use your spouse or others to delay dealing with fighting siblings—or anything else for that matter. Remember, the only guaranteed solution to negate all sibling rivalry is to only have one child.

Mama Drama Four: Lying

You find an empty Hershey bar wrapper in your daughter's room and chocolate smudges on the front of her skirt. When you ask her if she ate one of the chocolate bars you purchased to make s'mores with, she denies it. You know she's not telling the truth. What should you do?

1. Just ignore it. Everybody lies once in a while;
2. You say, "Okay, someone's in big trouble now. Who ate the chocolate bar?";
3. Don't ask if she ate it or not, because you know she did. Say something like, "Honey, I know you ate the chocolate bar without asking me first. What do you think I should do about that?"; or
4. Pretend like you believe her because you didn't actually see her eat the candy bar. Then keep your eye out for the next time she lies and you can more easily prove it.

Suggested Solutions

Lying is a common issue for preschool-age children, and although it is common, it is not something to ignore. In this situation a good approach is to calmly state what you know is true: she ate the candy bar without asking. Then without making accusations, calmly decide what you're going to do about it. Thus, the third option is a good immediate response.

Be careful how you phrase your questions in the heat of the moment. Without knowing it, you may be setting your daughter up to lie. What preschooler wants to be in big trouble? Threatening a child with punishment does not provide a good incentive to tell the truth. Also, rather than trying to catch a child doing something wrong, it's more effective to catch her doing something right. Praise her when she does tell the truth rather than being a suspicious parent who is always looking for your child's next lie. Scheduling a specific time to discuss lying with your child is a good idea, perhaps by having a family meeting especially about this topic rather than lecturing a child at the time of the lie.

Note: It is normal for two to five year olds to tell tall tales. When my middle son was five years old, he told lots of creative stories. One day he insisted he saw a bright green lizard in my friend's basement. No one believed him because he was always making up so many outrageous stories. Later that evening my friend called me and said a bright green lizard had indeed found its way into their basement. I told Jordan I was sorry for not believing him, but then we talked about the story of "the boy who cried wolf" and he seemed to understand why we didn't believe him. Usually, these tall tales are just a phase and not something to be concerned about.

Mama Drama Five: New Baby

At first your three year old seemed so excited about his new little sister, but a few days later he said he wanted her "to go back into your tummy." He's been acting out ever since. What can you do to help make this transition easier on both of you?

1. Make sure to give your older child your full attention a few times each day;
2. Tell your older child the baby needs you more than he does right now and he'll just have to get used to it;
3. Every time you sit down to nurse or feed the baby, ask the older child to do some chores for you; or
4. Assure and reassure your older child of your love, making him know no one can take his place.

Suggested Solutions

Bringing home a new baby and telling an older child to love and accept her is a little like your husband bringing home a new wife who's cuter and younger than you and telling you to love and accept her. Remembering this gives you some insight into how your older child might be feeling.

You can't tell a child enough how much you love him, and assure him that won't change with this new baby in the home.

It's a good idea to involve your older child in helping you, but if you ask him to do too much it will build resentment toward the baby. Gradually ask him to participate in helping with the baby. If you are afraid your older child might hurt the new baby, make sure to never leave them alone together.

If your older child regresses in some of his behavior, such as thumb-sucking or potty training, don't be alarmed or over-react. Lighten up your expectations on your older child to act "grown up" and know this is a phase that will pass.

Mama Drama Six: Not Listening

Your son doesn't listen to you. He seems to ignore everything you say. No matter how many times or how loudly you say something, he still doesn't respond. You're starting to wonder if something is wrong with his hearing. How can you get your son to listen better?

1. Talk calmly and make sure your requests are short and sweet;
2. Try a different mode of communication, such as a simple note or picture, to capture your child's attention and show him what you'd like him to do;
3. Take your son to a pediatrician and make sure his hearing is OK. He may have a chronic infection, wax buildup, or some other physical reason for poor hearing; or
4. Ask your child to repeat what you just said in his own words. This will help you know if he heard and understood you. Keep it brief.

Suggested Solutions

All of the above are good options to try when you feel your child isn't listening to you. Remember young children do not respond well to long explanations and detailed instructions. Your choice of words and tone of voice will have a huge impact on how your child receives what you are saying. Sometimes children will respond better to a different form of communication, such as singing, role-playing, or even drawing a simple picture to show your child what you want him to do. Try experimenting until you find the right approach to get your child's attention. This will also make your requests a little more fun. If you notice your child doesn't seem to hear others well, either, and you are concerned about a hearing problem, it is a good idea to have his hearing checked.

Listening is an important life skill, so make sure you model good listening. Your example will rub off on your child eventually. As Greek philosopher Epictetus said, "We have two ears and one mouth so that we can listen twice as much as we speak." Good advice.

Mama Drama Seven: Arguing

Your daughter argues with everything you say. It's driving you bonkers! How do you discourage this constant bickering?

1. Stick to your guns no matter what! You're the boss;
2. Let your child state her case without interrupting, and reconsider your decision;
3. Walk away and ignore your child;
4. Continue arguing until you prove you are right; or
5. You're sick and tired of arguing, so just give her what she wants. She'll outgrow this stage eventually.

Suggested Solutions

Children begin at an early age to negotiate when they do not get what they want. Negotiation is a good skill;

however, arguing serves no good purpose. A child who becomes good at arguing and ends up getting what she wants will continue this behavior as she gets older. Deal with it while they are young! If you find yourself constantly engaging in arguments with your child, here are some ideas to lessen the bickering.

When your child begins an argument, let her state her case. Let her talk without interrupting so she feels listened to. Then you can restate what you heard her say. Show a willingness at this point to reconsider your decision. If you are being unreasonable, it's okay to change your mind. However, if your decision still stands, calmly restate your decision after you've listened to your child. At this point the discussion can end. It's good to let your child know you will not engage in an argument about the subject. If the argument continues you may have to walk away or call a friend for support. Offering a distraction is always good too.

It takes two to argue. Try to remain firm and consistent, and do your best not to get sucked into an argument.

Mama Drama Eight: Potty Training

Potty training your daughter was no big deal. But with your son, it seems to be taking forever. What are some suggestions for getting this potty training over with?

1. Forget about "getting it over with" and work with your son's time frame, not your expectations or anyone else's;
2. Make potty training fun. Try putting Cheerios in the toilet and encourage your son to aim at them like targets;
3. You're definitely doing something wrong. Most kids are potty trained by the age of three, especially boys;

4. Don't stress about it. How many grown-ups do you know who are still not potty trained?; or

5. Options one, two, and four.

Suggested Solutions

Forcing a child to use the potty when he's not ready is not a good idea. It will result in power struggles and frustration for both parent and child. It's best to wait until a child shows signs of being interested in using the potty such as: disliking being in wet or poopy diapers, staying dry through a nap or bedtime, being curious about using the toilet, and expressing interest in not wearing a diaper.

Many people needlessly stress about this issue, but when you stop and think about it, how many adults are not potty trained? It will happen when your child is ready. Don't feel pressure from other parents or relatives, or compare your child to any other children. Most kids are potty trained sometime between the ages of three and five. However, some might struggle with staying dry through the night until age ten. It is also quite common for boys to take longer than girls. If you're really concerned, consult your physician. Sometimes something like a "potty pager," a wireless alarm used at night, can help (see www.pottypager.com). Expect accidents, because accidents do happen.

Most of all, keep potty training fun. Offer rewards, play potty games, and praise your child when he's successful. And don't flush your sense of humor down the toilet.

Mama Drama Nine: In-Laws' Unwanted Advice

Your in-laws keep making derogatory comments about how you swaddle your baby girl so snugly. "You might as well put her in a straitjacket. Don't bundle her up so tight," they say, along with other comments that make you feel inadequate. But you know it's the best way to calm her down, and she feels safe and secure. You're starting to get offended by their advice. What should you do?

1. It's your first baby and you really don't know what you're doing. Do what they say;
2. Be confident in knowing your own baby and her needs. Politely agree to disagree with their advice;
3. Remind them they grew up in a different generation and may have done things very differently than you; or
4. Tell your husband to talk to them about how their comments make you feel.

Suggested Solutions

First, trust your own instincts on knowing what your baby needs. If you truly are unsure, then try their suggestions. If the offensive comments become too irritating, approach them in such a way as to not cause permanent damage to your relationship. Be polite—and remember polite doesn't mean you have to embrace their unwanted advice.

A healthy grandparent/grandchild relationship is precious. If their comments become insulting, then talk to them. Or ask your husband to speak to them, depending on your relationship. If you don't feel you or your spouse can talk openly with them, then you might just have to let it go. Sometimes listening without arguing is a good choice, especially with family members whom you will interact with for many years.

Mama Drama Ten: Separation Anxiety

When you leave your son with the babysitter, he screams, cries, and clings to your leg. You have to pry his fingers off and run out the door. You feel awful leaving him. The babysitter says he's fine once you're gone, but you would like to help him (and you) handle these times of separation better. Any ideas?

1. It's probably the babysitter's fault. Try a new one;
2. Tell him you love him and you'll be back. Calmly pry his fingers off your leg, smile, wave goodbye, and go;
3. Just sneak out without saying goodbye and avoid the whole drama; or
4. Try having a fun activity planned for your babysitter to do with your son right after you leave. You can remind him once you're gone he gets to go to the park, or play with clay, or . . .

Suggested Solutions

Separation anxiety is experienced by most toddlers, and most outgrow this phase. Meanwhile, consistently reassure your little one that you will be back. Sneaking out is not a good idea. Many experts believe this causes feelings of being tricked and betrayed. It's a huge bummer for a child to look for a parent and then suddenly be told mom or dad is gone.

But there are some strategies you can try to make your leaving a little physically and emotionally smoother for both of you. First, don't freak out. Your reaction is contagious and will also be tested by your child. Be calm, be patient, and speak matter-of-factly. Verbally confirm your child's fears, but don't encourage the behavior. Second, don't drag out the drama. Tell your child you love him and you'll be back. Perhaps have a plan to do something fun together when you return. Say goodbye once, then turn around and leave. Don't hesitate and don't look back. Try having your child, your sitter, and you leave at the same time. They can go somewhere fun too.

Third, reassure your sitter that your child's behavior is not a response to them; rather this is normal behavior for young children. If it makes you feel better, give your sitter a call and see how your child is doing, without letting your child know you're doing this. Most children are fine once their parents are out of sight.

Did you have other solutions? Don't forget to share them, along with your own questions, at www.mops.org/mamadramas.

Practicing Your MomSense Section Summary

A friend recently said to me, "Practice does not make perfect. Practice makes progress." As a mom, I know I can't be perfect, and if that's the goal then I'm setting myself up for failure. If my goal is to make progress, then I'm heading down a road to success. Keep practicing the basic MomSense skills mentioned in this section: patience, respect, consistency, perspective, self-control, calm, joy, and love. And let's remember to adjust our mothering practices according to each child's needs and personalities.

If you're like me, you'll find it hardest to live out these positive qualities in the difficult times. But the more you practice these traits on a daily basis and build them into your family life, the more these behaviors will become a habit, a natural reaction to whatever life throws at you, and part of who you are and how you live. Oswald Chambers wrote, "If we will obey the Spirit of God, and practice in our physical life what God has placed within us by His Spirit, then when a crisis does come we will find that our own nature, as well as the grace of God, will stand by us."[2]

Section 3

Beyond Your MomSense

I am a little pencil in the hand of God who
is sending a love letter to the world.

Mother Teresa

I have a friend who shared something really interesting with
me. She lives in a community of young families with houses
situated fairly close to each other. Their neighborhood has
a community swimming pool, tennis courts, parks, walking
paths, and even a recreation center. It's an ideal place for
families to feel socially connected, something many of us
long for. Yet she said it doesn't feel that way.

Then she explained the "garage door" rule to me. She
said it's an unspoken tenet that if someone's garage door is
closed it means they don't want to socialize. If it's open, it's
a sign they are more willing to accept visitors. Most of the

time the garage doors are closed. Keeping the garage door closed is also part of their neighborhood covenant, but a closed door signified something much more to those living in this community.

My friend decided to do something about this. She started a Family Friday Afternoon Club. She opened her garage door every Friday afternoon, boldly breaking their neighborhood rule, set up tables with snacks and drinks, and invited everyone over. This drew neighbors and their kids to her home each week. They built relationships and grew closer as a neighborhood. At first she thought this was a small, insignificant thing to do, but it had a huge positive impact on her community.

As a woman named Betty Reese once said, "If you think you are too small to be effective, you have never been in bed with a mosquito." So true! I certainly don't want to have the negative impact on others that mosquitoes have in the world (one question on my list of things to ask God when I get to heaven: What was the purpose of the mosquito?), but we all can have a positive impact in the world when we do even the smallest acts for others—like opening our garage doors.

Social connectedness matters to our lives in the most significant ways. In *Bowling Alone: The Collapse and Revival of American Community,* author Robert D. Putnam writes that:

> [Extensive research] has established beyond reasonable doubt that social connectedness is one of the most powerful determents of our well-being. The more integrated we are with our community, the less likely we are to experience colds, heart attacks, strokes, cancer, depression, and premature death of all sorts. Such protective effects have been confirmed for close family ties, for friendship networks, for participation in social events and even for simple affiliation with religious and other civic associations.[1]

A woman with a healthy MomSense knows she needs others in her life, and she can initiate the process of creating community, build lasting relationships, and have a mind-set of doing life together, not alone.

That's what this next section is about: living beyond your own MomSense by relying on others, participating in authentic community, and having an enduring relationship with God—all of which can help you become a better mom—the mom your children need.

13

Created for Relationship

> God has not allowed us to see through each
> other, but to see each other through.
>
> *Unknown*

One year we took our boys on a surprise trip to California to visit Disneyland, Water World, and LEGOLAND. LEGO-LAND was paradise for our three boys. We were all amazed at life-size LEGO sculptures, a colorful park of seemingly endless LEGOs to build with, spouting water fountains, and even a little stream that allowed visitors to pan for gold. At one end of the park was a rollercoaster featuring a LEGO dinosaur. We rode the rollercoaster several times and then decided to head over to a play area so the two older boys, Josh and Jordan, could run around with Zane while I fed baby Jake. I assumed Jordan, our middle son, was with Zane—but

Zane assumed he was with me. Neither of us knew he had become separated from our family. He was lost, alone, and terrified in LEGOLAND.

After about fifteen minutes, I had just finished feeding Jake. Then I looked up and saw a woman wearing a green vest and khaki pants, the uniform worn by park staff, walking toward the play area holding Jordan's hand. Jordan's face was streaked with tears. My stomach flip-flopped. He saw me, released her hand, and flew into my arms. He wrapped his arms around my neck so tightly I could barely breathe, and I could tell he was trying not to cry. "Jordy, it's okay. What happened?"

He couldn't get the words out yet, so the woman answered, "I found him wandering around by himself by the stream where you can pan for gold. I let him do that for a while. I could tell he was getting worried, so we decided to walk around and look for you all."

"Thank you so much," I said. I was grateful, but felt awful for losing Jordan and not even knowing it. Zane and I had split up right near the little stream. Jordan had become enthralled and then distracted with the idea of finding gold. I went one way with Jake, Zane went the other way with Josh—and when Jordan looked around, he didn't see either of us. Zane and I had each assumed the other had Jordan. Picturing him in that instant made me feel horrible. I remember how terrifying it is to be lost and alone when you're a little kid. Don't you?

At some point in everyone's life, there is an experience or a memory of being alone. That awful feeling confirms to me that we were not created to be alone. We all have an innate need to be in relationship with others. Being alone is scary.

How does that relate to MomSense?

Simple. It's sensible to cultivate meaningful relationships. Now that we've discovered more about our own MomSense and practiced using and trusting it, it's time to expand and discover how we can learn from each other and walk together through motherhood. Our MomSense will grow when we're in relationship with others, and this will make us better moms who raise better kids and create a better world.

Developing a Strong Marriage/Parenting Partner

In the novel *Blessings* by Anna Quindlen, late one night a teenage couple drives up to a big white house, known as the Blessing estate, and leaves a baby in a cardboard box. The caretaker, Skip, finds the baby girl asleep and decides he wants to keep her. Lydia Blessing, the lonely, elderly matriarch of the estate, agrees to help him. Skip needs Lydia's help, and Lydia discovers her own blessings as she opens up her heart to Skip and the little girl he names Faith. This story is an excellent depiction of the resources a person finds in community. It's a powerful story of love, redemption, and personal change. Although it's fictional, it exemplifies a truth: raising children is best done in community—in authentic relationships with others. For many moms that other is a spouse, but if a spouse is not available then a strong parenting partner, like Skip and Lydia found in each other, is a key relationship to cultivate in the journey of parenting.

Research conducted by the YMCA and Search Institute revealed five key areas needed for successful parenting:

1. A support network
2. A healthy, growing marriage and/or strong parenting partner
3. A knowledge of basic mothering skills (MomSense)

4. Emotional resilience

5. A spiritual foundation and purpose for life[1]

"Historically, this parenting partner has been the husband or the child's father, but with the growing number of single mothers, other adults are stepping into this role," writes Shelly Radic in *Momology*.[2] Having two parents is still optimal for a child's well-being, but research also shows that, whether single or married, a supportive parenting partner makes raising a healthy, resilient child much easier.

Strong Marriage

If you are married and in the midst of raising little ones, it's crucial to not put this relationship on hold. Keep working on building a strong bond between you and your spouse.

Mom Story
Coffee Time

Someone told me, after we first had kids, to make sure to create time together as a couple. So Paul and I started having "coffee time" every evening after dinner. We'd tell the kids, "Mommy and Daddy are going to have coffee time and talk for a bit while you two play." The boys have become used to this and really respect our couple time together.

Then one day Noah came home from school and told me the cutest story. He said a girl in the class wanted him to be her boyfriend. "What did you say?" I asked.

"At first I didn't say anything." *Typical boy*, I thought. "Then when she asked me again, I told her

I couldn't be her boyfriend because I don't drink coffee."

I tried to keep myself from laughing. He was so serious. "What did she say then?" I asked.

"She said, 'Well that's okay, we don't have to drink coffee.'" He had never thought about this before. He assumed if you're someone's boyfriend that means you drink coffee together. He associated drinking coffee with something that bonds a couple together, because that's what he sees in our home.

I'm glad we've made it a point to do this and would recommend other couples find something like this to do together. It is good bonding for Paul and me, but it's also a good example for our kids to see us spending time together.

Michelle, mom of two

Spending valuable time together sometimes feels impossible with young children, but it isn't. Even if all you can manage is a daily fifteen-minute coffee time, it will do wonders for your marriage.

When our children were young, we were one of four couples that formed an informal co-op. We didn't call it a babysitting co-op because we were not that organized. Almost every week, one of the four couples would take all the children for an evening while the other couples went on dates. It was so much fun. Even the night of babysitting turned into a mini party. All the children had a blast together, and friendships blossomed. Even now, in their teenage years, this bunch of kids is close, almost cousin-like with each other. They are deeply committed to each other and involved in one another's lives—and so are we as their parents.

The memories are precious: games of hide and seek; water fights and food fights; tender moments of snuggling in their jammies, reading books, and silly games; shared jokes about the one couple who was always late in returning to pick up their kids, the couple who made all the kids eat cooked carrots, and the couple who were so desperate to go out they left their child with a broken arm are told and retold yet today. Getting one-on-one time with your husband does not have to be expensive, but whatever it takes to make this time part of your marriage is absolutely worth the effort.

Those of us who are married know a good marriage takes a lot of effort. Living intimately with another person eventually draws differences out into the open. We can't discuss marriage without discussing conflict. If a marriage is conflict-free, then the couple is either extremely blessed or in serious denial. Many times hardship wreaks havoc in a

Tips to Enhance Your Marriage Relationship

- Do something new together.
- Go on a date, but don't talk about the kids.
- Plan a romantic getaway.
- Write your spouse an encouraging note.
- Watch a funny movie.
- Schedule a regular date night.
- Plan ten minutes each day for the two of you to talk—uninterrupted.
- Take a cooking class together.
- Go for a walk.
- Volunteer together at the homeless shelter.
- Read a book together.
- Swap kids with other couples and plan inexpensive nights out.
- Be spontaneous together.

If you're feeling really disconnected from your spouse, you might want to seek marriage counseling. Contact a pastor at your local church and ask for suggestions for a good counselor. (Make sure to get references.) Keeping your family intact is worth the hard work of making your marriage work.

marriage. Unemployment, illness, unfaithfulness, control issues, unmet expectations, money, communication, in-laws, toddlers, teenagers, moving, and so many other factors affect a couple. Rather than working together during hard times, many couples work against each other or even without each other.

Shauna Niequist, in her book *Bittersweet: Thoughts on Change, Grace, and Learning the Hard Way*, describes a challenging time in her marriage. She and her husband, Aaron, experienced having to abruptly leave their jobs and close relationships at a large church. "Instead of walking together through the mess, talking and listening, learning and hearing, Aaron and I squared off like boxers, demanding and bickering and then eventually just ignoring each other."[3] Ultimately they learned to hear and understand each other and move forward together, but difficult times like these can leave scars if a husband and wife hurt each other. A couple is meant to be stronger together, but it takes work. It's not easy, but it is best.

DadSense

Talking to moms about this book, I heard numerous accounts about how hard it is for many moms to trust their husbands' common sense when it comes to their children. My friend Tessa, like many moms, has experienced both being right in her MomSense and also needing to trust her husband's DadSense. When her first baby, Neal, was born and they were still in the hospital, Neal cried inconsolably. Her husband, Jeff, decided Neal was too hot, all wrapped up in the baby blankets. Tessa assured him the baby wasn't too hot, but he insisted. So she gave in. They unwrapped the little bundle to let him cool down. A while later, the nurse came in and took the baby's temperature. "He's too cold," the nurse announced.

"We need to warm him up." Tessa gave Jeff a look to say "I told you so." Jeff knew he had been wrong. They placed the baby under heat lamps and had Tessa hold him close, skin to skin, until he warmed up.

Later, Jeff asked, "How did you know he wasn't too hot?" Tessa didn't really have words to describe how she knew; she just sensed that wasn't what was bothering him. Jeff grew to trust Tessa's instincts and committed to developing his own.

When their second baby, Luke, was born, Tessa was a hormonal mess when they brought him home from the hospital. She couldn't make any decisions, even what type or how many noodles to cook for pasta, so she cooked all the noodles they had in their cupboard. And to make matters worse, Neal didn't like the idea of the new little guy. He was angry, jealous, acting out, and not letting either parent hug him. Thankfully, Jeff's DadSense kicked in. He told Tessa he was taking Neal for a walk.

> The beauty of the mom and dad combination is that when balance between the two different individuals is achieved, it creates a sense of completeness.

Jeff plopped Neal into the stroller and started wandering around the neighborhood. He knew Neal needed assurance of their love. Tessa was too much of a wreck at the moment to see and do that, and she needed to take care of Luke and herself. As Jeff meandered around, he would stop the stroller and kneel in front of his son, eye to eye, and say, "I love you. Mommy and I love you." Finally, after about twenty times of hearing this, Neal reached out his arms and let Jeff scoop him up in a bear hug. Neal got it. From that moment on, Neal didn't feel threatened. He knew he was loved, and he adjusted to the new baby in the family.

Tessa speaks tenderly of Jeff's intervention in this moment. She saw his DadSense kick in, perhaps because her Mom-Sense was at such a low point, and this moment helped her become more confident in her husband. He, like her, knew what he was doing.

As difficult as it might be, it's best to allow your children and their dad to have their own relationships. What he brings into the relationship with his DadSense will complement what you bring with your MomSense. Research has proven that children benefit the most from healthy relationships with both a mother and a father. Combine the positive influences of both mom and dad, male and female, and the result will most likely be a well-rounded child who knows how to relate to both his parents. And these children have a better chance for successful relationships in the future.

Many times we moms are so intuitive to our children's needs it's hard to let go of what we know and trust our spouse (or anyone else) to have the same awareness. But if we never let our husbands experience that, or if we correct and criticize them, then our husbands won't grow in their confidence as dads.

Dad Story

A Daddy's Priorities

Recently I had a wake-up call. Actually, it was more of a wake-up scream.

It had been a dismal morning. In one hand was a stack of bills, in the other was my checkbook, and the two did not meet in the middle. I also had a list of emails marked urgent and a list of honey-dos taped to the fridge, the house was messy, and the coffeepot died before breakfast.

Now, I'm a fairly optimistic guy, and any one of these things would not typically depress me, but cumulatively the load was feeling huge and heavy. I spent the morning staring at my computer screen and worrying.

That's when my two year old, who was napping, screamed.

It was a scream I'd never heard from her before, not frustration or even fear, but pain.

I was out of my chair in a heartbeat, and all my previous worries suddenly disappeared. Nothing else mattered except ensuring my girl was okay.

Luckily, it was nothing more than her leg becoming trapped in the slats of her crib when she tried to roll over in her sleep. Ten minutes in the rocking chair and a sippy-cup of milk later, she was back asleep, safe and sound.

Still, in the few seconds that it took me to get from my desk to her door, I experienced a blinding flash of the obvious. Bills would be paid, or they wouldn't—we weren't going to starve. Chores would be done, or not—and there was always next weekend. Nothing on my worry list was more than a B priority at best, and my A priority had needed my help. Nothing could have kept me from rescuing my screaming daughter.

An hour later, I still hadn't made much of a dent in any of the lists, but when my daughter woke up for real, I put a pair of sandals on her, turned off the computer, and went with her to the park to play.

Perry, dad of one

Moms, if we believe "mom always knows best," we might be wrong. Let's do an experiment and give our husbands a chance to grow in their DadSense as we sit back, keep our mouths shut, and watch the father-child relationship bloom.

Strong Parenting Partner

If you are divorced, never married, widowed, or in a complicated marriage or relationship and the child's father is not interested in being your partner in parenting, then find someone who is.

Research suggests having a strong parenting partner is essential to successful mothering. A parenting partner can be a mom, aunt, sister, mom-in-law, cousin, friend, or whoever will come alongside and help you. Shelly Radic describes this concept well.

> A parenting partner relationship should provide practical support to fulfill the day-to-day responsibilities of caring for a child as well as emotional support such as a listening ear or a break when you're tired. Mental support is also important; a partner can help research things like day care options and health issues. Finally, a parenting partner can provide spiritual support, praying for your child and modeling a strong relationship with God.[4]

Partnering with someone else is not only helpful to you as a mom, but is also beneficial to your children. Interacting with another adult, learning to respect his or her influence, and developing a special relationship with this other person will have a long-lasting, positive impact on children.

The Search Institute has identified forty developmental assets for early childhood that help young children grow up healthy, caring, and responsible. These practical things have an enduring influence on children. Rather than focusing on problems, the Search Institute's research concentrates on the positive things all people need. Instilling these forty building blocks in a child's life can help him or her make wise decisions and choose a positive lifestyle. Several of those building blocks for success discuss the need children have for support from family, friends, and community who "provide the child with high levels of consistent and predictable love, physical care, and positive attention in ways that are responsive to the child's individuality."[5]

Another asset mentioned is encouraging our children to develop other adult relationships, because this gives our children experience with caring adults outside the family. Sometimes we love best by letting someone else take the load for a while. Sometimes we love best by helping our children see they are valued not just by us, but by others as well. All forty of these assets are worth building in your own family, and I highly recommend visiting www.search-institute.org, printing up these assets, and placing them somewhere very visible in your home.

Mothering in partnership with another person brings a much-needed shoulder to lean on for support, emotionally and physically, and will result in well-adjusted children.

Friends Don't Let Friends Mother Alone

One of my favorite stories in the Bible is about four friends who undertake drastic measures to get their paralyzed friend to see Jesus. First, they carried him on a stretcher for who knows how long to reach the home where Jesus was speaking. When they finally arrived, it was so crowded there was no room for anyone to get in the house—or even near the door. So these friends climbed up on the roof and dug a hole through it. In these days, roofs were made of concrete-like mud, two to three feet thick. Digging this hole was not easy. Who knows if they came prepared with the tools they needed—such as ladders, ropes, and digging implements—or if they found them nearby, but whatever they needed to do, they did. These men had relentless determination, desperate to help their friend. How they must have loved him.

Imagine the scene in the home. As Jesus spoke, the crowd might have heard scraping and digging noises coming from above. At some point, flecks of dust and sprinkles of dirt rained down on the crowd—even on Jesus's head. Then chunks of dirt might have come crashing down, suddenly revealing a large hole in the roof that allowed bright, hot sunlight to pour in. Next, blocking the light, a stretcher-like bed probably held by ropes slowly descended from the hole in the roof to the feet of Jesus. I would have loved to witness this in person. I think Jesus might have had a huge smile on his face as he looked up and saw the four men's faces anxiously peering down at him from the hole.

Then the Bible says, "When Jesus saw their faith," *their faith*, the faith of this man's friends, he completely healed the paralytic emotionally, spiritually, and physically. The man rose to his feet, picked up his bed, and left. Everyone was amazed and said, "We have never seen anything like this!" (see Mark 2:1–12).

My guess is the healed man ran to find his friends, and tears streaked their dirt-covered faces as they hugged and celebrated with him.

Imagine if our modern-day friendships mirrored this. We, as moms, can carry each other through life's ups and downs. Sometimes we might be the one who needs to be carried to Jesus; sometimes we are the stretcher carriers and roof diggers, relentless in helping our friends. Because of our love and determination to make sure no one mothers alone, the world will say, "We have never seen anything like this!"

Girlfriends Are Good for Your Health

Did you know that not having close friends is as detrimental to your health as smoking? A nurses' health study from Harvard Medical School found that the more friends women have, the less likely they are to develop physical impairments as they age, and the more likely they are to lead joyful lives. The results were so significant that the researchers concluded that not having close friends or confidants was as detrimental to your health as smoking or carrying extra weight.[6] Friends are proven to be good for your health, and thus are good for your family's health. In the craziness of raising children it can feel overwhelming to make time for friends, but this is one area worth pushing past your circumstances to find time for. If it means you have to give up unloading your dishwasher or doing another load of laundry (hard choices, I know), choose the friend time.

When I had toddlers, one friend and I would meet in the late afternoons just before dinner, because this time of day was especially challenging for me. We jokingly called it "Happy Hour" because we, and our kids, were usually anything but happy. My kids were stir-crazy, Zane wouldn't be home for dinner for a while, and my patience for the day was wearing out. This friend and I would regularly meet at a park, go for a walk or swim, or meet at a coffee shop that had a sandbox. This time with her made the unbearable part of my day fun. I looked forward to seeing her. Our kids played together while we talked. When we got home for dinner, I didn't feel quite so burned out. Rather than wanting to hand the kids over to Zane when he came home and bolt for a few hours, I had the energy and the good attitude I needed to make the rest of our night much more pleasant—and the kids tired and ready for bed earlier.

I know women's friendships can be complicated and sometimes even painful. Knowing when to make a new friend, working through an issue with a friend, or even saying "so long" to a toxic friendship can all cause us lots of angst. But having and keeping friends can be a woman's sanity, especially in the early mothering years. Authentic friendships, where women are honest and vulnerable, create a sense of closeness and commitment.

No one friend is going to be perfect. I love what author Barbara Kingsolver has to say about friends: "The friend who holds your hand and says the wrong thing is made of dearer stuff than the one who stays away." Friends who offer each other grace and show commitment to one another, no matter what, will give a woman a precious gift in life: a true friend.

Mothering together, learning, and sometimes relying on each other's MomSense brings growth, a sense of belonging, and comfort to a woman in the midst of the mommy whirlwind.

MomSense from Other Mothers

How has being involved in a mom group helped you?

It's one of the best things I've ever done real friends, real life. –Holly, mom of two

It's a place to meet other mommies who are going through the same challenges, heartaches, celebrations, and frustrations as you are. A place you can be yourself and know that you are not alone. –Chelsea, mom of two

It's my happy, refueling time. –Charlotte, mom of two

One of the moms in my group calls it her sanity check. I call it my safety net. —Sandra, mom of one

To find your own mom group, call a local church or visit www.MOPS.org.

It's a great way to meet mothers and form friendships. —Janelle, mom of one

Mentors

Having a woman in your life who is a little bit ahead of you in years and/or experience is invaluable. A while back I coauthored a book of older women's stories intended to encourage younger women and to motivate them to have intergenerational friendships. In conducting research for our book, my coauthor and I discovered many women longed for a mentor but didn't have that type of relationship—myself included. I was also going through an extremely difficult time and had been praying God would bring a more mature woman into my life with whom I could seek advice and find friendship. Then one day at the gym, Judy, who is about fifteen years older than me and further along in the journey of marriage and raising kids, came over to say hello. Because we knew many of the same people, she was aware of the difficulties I was facing. After a few minutes of polite chat she simply asked, "Is there anything I can do for you?"

"Would you like to get together every once in a while?" I asked. "I've been wanting to meet with another woman for advice."

"I'd love to get together," she exclaimed. "And I've been praying for a prayer partner—would you like to pray together too?"

We started getting together regularly to talk and pray. And thirteen years later, we still get together. I can talk with Judy about anything. She is genuine, trustworthy, and faithful. She has shared openly with me, and her experiences have helped guide me as I've come up against similar situations. Her wisdom has helped me make decisions. Her example has inspired me in my own life. Her relationship with her husband and children speaks volumes to me in how I want to relate to my own family.

One of my favorite stories about my relationship with Judy is a time when she asked me to go on a fifty-mile bike ride. I had been biking regularly, so I thought, *No big deal.* The morning of our ride I got my bike ready, filled up my water bottle, pocketed a granola bar, and at the last minute grabbed a light rain jacket.

We were riding to a small town called Gold Hill in the foothills above Boulder, Colorado. As we rode our way up the steep, paved road, I found myself looking down at the white painted line on the side of the asphalt. Judy would cheerfully remind me to look around and enjoy the view. About halfway up, I finished off my water bottle and ate my granola bar. I had no idea how far we had to go or what to expect for the rest of the ride, and steel-gray rain clouds were gathering above us. She made comments to encourage me, such as "Around this corner the road levels off a bit." She knew exactly what was coming. When we finally reached the little town, we took a short break to enjoy the breathtaking views and have a snack, but as I mentioned I had already gulped down my granola bar. Judy, however, had packed extra food and an orange that she shared with me. The rain started to sprinkle on us, and we decided we had better hurry up and get back to Boulder before it became a major downpour.

Unfortunately, we weren't fast enough. Within a few minutes, the rain clouds let loose and quickly soaked us. I started shivering and wondered if my cell phone would work from this point. I was about to check. If I had service, I was going to call Zane and beg him to come pick us up. Judy pulled over to the side of the road and waited until I caught up to her. Then she reached in her little pack on her bike and pulled out two pairs of rain pants, headbands, and gloves. Not only was she prepared for herself, she had me in mind when she packed that morning. She knew—because she had done this ride many times before. She also knew I was pretty clueless, so she came prepared to help me. And that is typical of our relationship.

If you asked Judy, she would tell you our friendship is mutually beneficial and an answer to both our prayers, but I really think I have the better end of the deal. I don't have words to express how grateful I am for her friendship and guidance. I hope and pray you will seek—and find—a mentor who will speak love, wisdom, and faithfulness into your life.

Your MomSense

- As moms, sometimes we crave time alone and that's healthy—but do you ever feel like you're mothering alone? If yes, jot down two specific steps you can take to engage in community:

- On a scale of one to ten, one being very disconnected and ten being very close, where would you rate yourself in terms of your relationship with your husband?
- If you're not married, do you have someone in your life who is a strong parenting partner? If not, what steps can you take to begin creating this type of relationship?
- Do you have a more experienced woman you can talk to and get advice from? If yes, send her a note reminding her how much you value that relationship. If no, write down what characteristics you would look for in a woman you would like to have as a mentor:

_____

_____

- Finding a mentor can feel intimidating, but don't be afraid to ask someone you admire if she would be willing to meet with you. Most older women feel intimidated too, but are honored when asked.

14

Sensing Something Greater

Dare I really let God be to me all that He says He will be?

Oswald Chambers[1]

Becoming a mother opens up a new window in a woman's mind and heart. Maybe it's that cute cherubic face smiling up at her, or the overwhelming feeling of love and a sense of responsibility, that lead a mom to experience a newfound longing for God in her life. This unique slice of time in a woman's life leads many moms to go to church and find out more about God.

The Baylor Survey of Religion looked at Americans' religious beliefs and practices and found the following:

- The average mother is 21 percent more likely to attend religious services at least twice a month, compared to similar women who do not have children.

- Even a parent (male or female) who is lacking in religious beliefs is about 50 percent more likely to attend religious services twice a month or more, compared to similar people without children.
- At a minimum, parents are a lot more likely to go to church than people with no children.[2]

The researchers also described the dramatic positive effect on children when parents take their children to church: "Children from more religious families and from families with higher rates of religious attendance are better behaved and more well adjusted at home and at school."[3]

Expert Opinion

Why Faith Is Good for the Family

The Barna Research Group has found that intentionally raising children with spirituality will more likely result in them becoming adults who possess a strong faith and live out their beliefs in tangible ways. Also, Focus on the Family has found that many children begin their relationship with Jesus by asking him into their hearts when they are preschoolers, so taking advantage of this window in a child's life helps moms raise God-loving children.

We as parents have been given a powerful charge by a God who promises to come alongside us as we navigate the unpredictable challenges that parenting presents. This comes from the authentic relationship that we have with Jesus.

So then, how do we do this?

Raising children spiritually starts with our own relationship with God. Talking about our faith with our children and modeling biblical values in our own lives will help them begin to see how vital God is to our existence and theirs. What is that like? Do we regularly read the Bible? Do we take time to pray? Do we have people who support our faith and spiritual growth? Becoming involved with a church community can help. When we are around others who love God and encourage us to live that way, it promotes both our own personal growth and has a positive effect on the spiritual growth of our children.

Liz Selzer, PhD in Education Training and Performance Improvement, MDiv and MA

But let's take faith to a more personal level. We know going to church is good for the kids, but what about you, mom?

Sensing God

Do you ever feel like you're part of something much bigger than what you actually see? Every once in a while when I actually have time to ponder bigger, deeper thoughts (which isn't very often), I have a sense of something greater going on than what I see in my daily life.

I look around and see others—so many others. I see the mom down the street pushing her baby in a stroller with her pet pug waddling along beside them. I see my ninety-year-old neighbor sitting on his front porch in his red and green flannel pajamas, reading his morning newspaper. I see the college-age girl behind the coffee counter with the serpent tattoo on her forearm serving me my chai tea latte. I see the homeless man begging on the corner, and I can't help but wonder if his mom knows. I see my mom, dad, and sisters sitting around a dining room table, telling recent vacation stories. I see my nieces and nephews razzing each other and planning their future adventures. I see Zane sitting on the couch in his office plucking away at his guitar. I see my boys, each resembling a little bit of Zane and a little bit of me. And I have a sense something great is going on—and I'm a part of it.

My sense of God is growing, due to all the amazing people in my life.

I see miracles everywhere, every day. I watch the sun rise and set. I see and feel the sky release cold, fluffy snow that blankets my world. I observe flowers that tenderly open their petals when the sun shines on them and serenely close each night. I see swarms of purple butterflies on the trails where I hike near our home. I see birds swoop down to play in the puddles of water left on our sidewalk after a rainstorm. I eat cherries from the tree in our backyard. And I start to feel I am definitely part of something beautiful and big.

My sense of God helps me see beauty where I didn't see it before.

Recently, we visited the Grand Canyon. Standing on the cliff of a popular lookout spot, I felt awe. I watched my boys scramble around on the rocks and pose for pictures in front of this magnificent scene and thought, *There's no way this happened by accident.* The beauty, the depth, the colors, the immensity of this spectacular place, and the people sharing it with me made me more certain than ever that there is a God and I am a part of his bigger purpose and plan.

My growing sense of God allows me to notice evidence of him around me all the time. Just think about the amazing human body. The intricacy of each human being is really beyond comprehension. Did you know:

- The lungs contain 300,000 capillaries. If laid end to end they would stretch 1500 miles.
- Human bone is as strong as granite in supporting weight.
- Each finger- and toenail takes six months to grow from base to tip.
- Each kidney contains one million individual filters. They filter an average of 2.2 pints of blood per minute.
- The focusing muscles of the eyes move around 100,000 times a day. To give your leg muscles the same workout you would need to walk fifty miles per day.
- In thirty minutes the average body gives off enough heat to bring one half gallon of water to boil.

- A single human blood cell takes only sixty seconds to make a complete circuit of the body.[4]
- Scientists have counted more than five hundred liver functions.
- The left lung is bigger than the right lung to make room for the heart.
- Every person has a unique tongue print.
- A sneeze zooms out of your mouth at more than one hundred miles per hour.
- The tooth is the only part of the human body that can't repair itself.[5]

These facts about the human body make me even more certain that a loving God created us. The uniqueness of every individual mother, father, and child is remarkable. Beyond. Words.

Living beyond your MomSense is partly about recognizing that you are important and part of something bigger, and growing in your sense of God. You have not been created to live alone. You have been created for relationship.

However, as we live in community with others and in relationship with those we love, we still might feel empty. A nagging part of us still feels something is missing. No one person, cause, or event has been able to satisfy that hunger for more—except a relationship with God.

I believe there is something *more*. Do you sense it too?

I believe God created this world and every single living animal and person in it. I believe he wants to have a relationship with us—a loving, completely accepting relationship. Evidence of his unconditional love surrounds us all the time, and he's reaching out to us to become our friend—to give us what we need to mother and develop our MomSense.

How? Through Jesus.

Jesus, God's Son, lived on this earth and experienced life as a human. He experienced it all—the joy, the sorrow, the pleasure, and the pain life throws at us. He lived in a human body. His heart pumped a single blood cell through his body in sixty seconds. His liver performed more than five hundred functions. His sneezes were more than one hundred miles per hour too. He lived out the characteristics listed in this book: love, joy, calm, patience, respect, consistency, and self-control. He definitely had the big picture in mind and lived for what mattered most.

And he lived in community. He spent time getting to know people, healing the sick, and giving sight to the blind. He fed hungry people and hung out with the outcasts (that included women, by the way). He spoke up for justice and criticized hypocrites. He loved children and invited them to sit with him and hear his stories. He told amazing stories that changed people's lives. He lived love. And he loved completely, without ever sinning. That love led to death on a cross as the ultimate sacrifice for the world's sins, opening the door for us to have a relationship with God.

If you're sensing God and want to know him more deeply, consider talking to him about that. You can say a prayer that goes something like this:

> Jesus, I want to know you. Please fill this emptiness I have inside. I've tried on my own and I cannot do it. I need your help. I believe you did what you did because you want to know me. Come into my life and help me become the woman you created me to be. Amen.

Tell a friend, find a faith community, read the Bible, and begin to grow in the most exciting relationship ever. Like any relationship, you grow closer to God as you get to know each other.

To Get to Know God Better

- join a Christian church
- attend a Bible study
- find authentic friends to help you
- find a Christian mentor
- read the Bible, God's love letter to you
- pray often—talk to him like your best friend
- feed the hungry
- visit the sick
- love the unlovable
- ask someone about the Holy Spirit
- don't give up
- be devoted to growth
- trust God with the big and little things in life
- look hopefully toward your future
- keep a journal recording what God does for you
- observe your child's faith
- trust in God more than in yourself
- keep God at the center of your life

The Next Thing

It's time to take what we've learned about our unique Mom-Sense and begin daily and boldly to be a better mom, one who is close to others and who trusts in God.

Mothers have a huge influence on society and play a key role in shaping culture. "There is no more significant group of culture changers in the world than mothers," said bestselling author Rick Warren during his keynote speech at the 2004 MOPS International Convention. It's true! We can change the world, one day at a time. Our influence on our children, spouses, extended family, and community will have a ripple effect. Everything we do and every person we influence matters. Let's live confidently, knowing moms do matter and we truly can make this world an amazing place.

Put your MomSense and sense of God into action so you can be the mother your children need and the woman the world needs.

Etcetera

All life is an experiment. The more experiments the better.

Ralph Waldo Emerson

Like life, mothering is a series of experiments. It's a whole lot of trying—sometimes succeeding, sometimes failing—and then trying some more.

Discovering and practicing our MomSense, expanding our MomSense knowledge, and living beyond our MomSense in close relationships with God and others will continue throughout the different seasons of our lives. The MomSense we're discovering today will be part of us forever and will continually grow and change—as we will too.

What we've learned so far about ourselves, about decision making—and about creating a parenting philosophy based on the big, underlying character traits of healthy families—is all to be taken in and spilled out over and over again. We'll keep learning new bits and pieces along the way; the process of mothering never stops. We have continual opportunities to grow together as we develop individually through our experiments and share our successes and failures with each other.

The Forever Bond of Mothers

I recently watched the movie *Babies*, a brilliant documentary about the first year of four babies in four different countries. Even though the babies' cultures, their experiences, and the parenting practices of their moms were radically different, the sense of connectedness I felt with these four mommies was astounding. MomSense exists in all moms everywhere.

Moms have a common understanding of the love, demands, joys, and challenges of raising children. We immediately connect with each other because we know all moms need their MomSense just like we do. We are of the same tribe, bound by a commonality beyond our immediate circumstances. Wherever we live and whatever we do; whether we are married or not; whatever skin, hair, or toenail color we have; an understanding exists between all moms—including the two moms in the following story, who found themselves in a very scary situation.

Mom Story
Flight 1549

I wrestled my carry-on into the luggage rack above my seat on my flight from New York, bound for Charlotte, North Carolina. Exhausted from a fast and furious work trip, I looked forward to seeing my husband and three children. As I glanced down, about to squeeze into my seat, I noticed a light blue baby blanket draped across the back of my chair. I took the blanket, felt the soft material between my thumb and forefinger, and handed it to the flight attendant, who then passed it to a woman who was holding a baby in the rear galley area.

Sitting in my spot in the last row of the airplane, I ate a snack and received phone calls from both my husband and my sister while waiting for the other passengers to board and the plane to take off. I chuckled at my husband's important question about what kind of dog food to buy our new dog. Little did I know I was about to experience one of the most terrifying events in my life.

Finally, the airplane backed away from the gate, taxied down the runway, and took off. Very shortly into the ascent I heard a "BOOM!" Startled, I looked at my seatmate, who was looking out the window, and asked, "What was that?"

"It was a bird," he answered.

Then I smelled and saw smoke coming from the left side of the plane. The engine noise stopped. An eerie silence filled the plane. I knew something was terribly wrong. I stifled a scream and my heart began beating so loudly I'm sure the man next to me could hear it. About that time the captain's voice echoed throughout the quiet plane: "This is the captain. Brace for impact."

Holding my head tight to my knees, I immediately thought of my children. *If I die who will plan their weddings or birthday parties?* I was convinced I was not going to survive. It all happened so fast. The plane went down and hit the water. The captain had made a quick, calculated decision to land on the Hudson River. I heard a splash and the sound of water rushing past. I remember being astonished at how smooth the crash landing was. *I'm alive. Unbelievable,* I thought.

I ripped off my seatbelt and bolted to the rear of the plane, the nearest exit. When I got to the galley, the flight attendant had cracked open the rear left side door but it would not open all the way because of the water pressure. I went over and tried to help her push the door but it wouldn't open beyond a crack. I went over to the right side rear door and it wouldn't budge either. Water was rushing in through the cracked door and the flight attendant hollered, "We're in the water, go to the wings!" She looked at me and said, "We have two minutes." She then left the rear galley and bolted up the aisle.

By this time the ice cold water in the galley had risen up to my chest. I had survived the crash but now feared I might drown. I looked up and people were still coming toward the rear galley. I put both hands up and began saying "Go to the wings, go to the wings, we can't get out back here, go to the wings." People began to hear, understand, and start turning around. I kept chanting the same thing over and over. Somehow I managed to move through the deep water toward another exit door that was open. I could see people getting out.

"We're going to make it, keep going, we're going to live," I said out loud, thrilled to see the door getting closer and closer.

I was one of the last to exit the plane and stand on the wing, the dark gray water of the river flowing below us. People were already in an emergency raft and that's when I saw her, the mom from earlier. She stood rigidly, holding her baby in one arm with her little girl clinging to her hand on her other side. The little girl hugged the blue blanket that had been on my seat.

I heard people from the boat screaming, "Throw the baby!" Now, this captured my attention. My Mom-Sense kicked in. I knew that was not a good idea, and I knew that this mother was not going to toss her baby into the boat after surviving a plane crash. She needed my help. I guess you could say that I shifted into "Mommy mode," and I stepped onto the back left edge of the raft, one foot on the raft and one foot on the wing of the plane. I looked at the terrified mother and gently coaxed, "Give me your baby." A moment of understanding passed between us, like she knew I was a mommy too and she could trust me. She handed me her baby and I passed him to a man seated safely in the raft. I then looked at the mother and said, "Now give me your little girl." She passed me her daughter and I sat down on the back edge of the raft with the girl in my lap.

During the ten or fifteen minutes that we sat on the life raft waiting for the ferry boat to get positioned appropriately to begin the rescue, I rubbed the little girl's head and told her how brave she was and that we were going to be okay. I knew what my own children would need in the circumstance. The bond I felt with this other mom was amazing. We could understand each other's hearts, fears, children's needs, and so much more I can't even put into words, it was just knowing.

Vallie, mom of three

Vallie and the other mom on the airplane immediately related to each other; a sense of trust and understanding existed between them. Vallie's MomSense radar detected the concerns and needs of the mom who had her children with her on the crashed airplane, and Vallie went into mom-mode to help the other woman in the way only another mom could.

I believe that we live extraordinary lives as moms. My hope and prayer is that you live bravely, lovingly, intuitively,

185

sensibly, and securely in your role as mom. And I hope and pray you always trust that God will help you become the mom he made you to be, and that you will believe you are the mom your children need.

As you move forward, trust your MomSense—because you do know more than you think you do.

Notes

Introduction

1. Marisa De Los Santos, *Love Walked In* (New York: Penguin Group, 2005), 107.
2. Martha Farrell Erickson and Enola G. Aird, "The Motherhood Study: Fresh Insights on Mothers' Attitudes and Concerns" (Institute for American Values, 2005), www.motherhoodproject.org.

Chapter 2 Mom and You

1. Henry Cloud and John Townsend, *The Mom Factor: Dealing with the Mother You Had, Didn't Have, or Still Contend With* (Grand Rapids: Zondervan, 1996), 12–13.
2. Dave Carder, Earl Henslin, John Townsend, Henry Cloud, and Alice Brawand, *Secrets of Your Family Tree: Healing for Adult Children of Dysfunctional Families* (Chicago: Moody Press, 1991), 160–61.
3. Donald Miller, *A Million Miles in a Thousand Years* (Nashville: Thomas Nelson, 2009), 29.

Chapter 3 What's a Mama to Do?

1. Barry Schwartz, *The Paradox of Choice: Why More Is Less* (New York: Harper Collins, 2004), 20.
2. Shelly Radic, *Momology: A Mom's Guide to Shaping Great Kids* (Grand Rapids: Revell, 2010), 75–76.
3. Schwartz, *Paradox of Choice*, 85–86.
4. Jonah Lehrer, *How We Decide* (New York: Mariner, 2010), 15.
5. Ibid., 143–44.

6. See www.sleep-deprivation.com and www.healthysleep.med.harvard.edu.
7. Katherine Ellison, *The Mommy Brain: How Motherhood Makes Us Smarter* (New York: Basic Books, 2005), 52.
8. Ibid., 125.

Chapter 4 Sense of Patience

1. *Merriam-Webster's Collegiate Dictionary*, eleventh edition.
2. Copyright © 2001 by *Christianity Today International/Christian Parenting Today Magazine*. Reprinted by permission of Christianity Today International, www.christianitytoday.com.

Chapter 5 Sense of Respect

1. Michele Borba, *12 Simple Secrets Real Moms Know: Getting Back to the Basics and Raising Happy Kids* (San Francisco: Jossey-Bass, 2006), 107–8.

Chapter 6 Sense of Consistency

1. Kevin Leman, *Have a New Kid by Friday: How to Change Your Child's Attitude, Behavior, and Character in 5 Days* (Grand Rapids: Revell, 2008), 54.

Chapter 8 Sense of Self-Control

1. Ellen Galinsky, *Mind in the Making: The Seven Essential Life Skills Every Child Needs* (New York: Harper Studio, 2010), 26.
2. Ibid., 65.

Chapter 10 Sense of Joy

1. Melinda Smith, Gina Kemp, and Jeanne Segal, "Laughter is the Best Medicine: The Health Benefits of Humor and Laughter," Helpguide.org, http://helpguide .org/life/humor_laughter_health.htm.
2. Lisa T. Bergren and Rebecca Price, *What Women Want: The Life You Crave and How God Satisfies* (Colorado Springs: Waterbrook Press, 2007), 156.
3. Elisa Morgan, *Naked Fruit: Getting Honest about the Fruit of the Spirit* (Grand Rapids: Revell, 2004), 68–69.

Chapter 11 Sense of Love

1. Tom Rath and Donald O. Clifton, *How Full Is Your Bucket? Positive Strategies for Work and Life* (New York: Gallup Press, 2004), 15.

Chapter 12 Mama Dramas

1. You may have your own ideas and creative responses for these scenarios, or there may be other issues about which you'd like some advice. Please post your questions and solutions on www.mom-ology.org/finesse, and join other moms in honest conversation regarding specific mama dramas.

2. Oswald Chambers, *My Utmost for His Highest* (Uhrichsville: Barbour, 1935), July 7.

Section 3 Beyond Your MomSense

1. Robert D. Putnam, *Bowling Alone: The Collapse and Revival of American Community* (New York: Simon & Schuster, 2000), 326.

Chapter 13 Created for Relationship

1. YMCA and Search Institute, "Building Strong Families: A Preliminary Study on American Parents and Resources They Need to Succeed" (November 2002), http://www.search-institute.org/families.

2. Radic, *Momology*, 167.

3. Shauna Niequist, *Bittersweet: Thoughts on Change, Grace, and Learning the Hard Way* (Grand Rapids: Zondervan, 2010), 25.

4. Radic, *Momology*, 167–68.

5. Jolene L. Roehlkepartain and Nancy Leffert, *A Leader's Guide to What Young Children Need to Succeed: Working Together to Build Assets from Birth to Age 11* (Minneapolis: Free Spirit, 2000), 77.

6. "UCLA Study On Friendship Among Women," Gale Berkowitz, *Melissa Kaplan's Chronic Neuroimmune Diseases*, last modified December 19, 2009, http://www.anapsid.org/cnd/gender/tendfend.html.

Chapter 14 Sensing Something Greater

1. Chambers, *My Utmost for His Highest*, July 9.

2. Rodney Stark, *What Americans Really Believe* (Waco: Baylor University Press, 2008), 183.

3. Ibid., 184.

4. "Top 15 Amazing Facts About the Human Body," *Listverse: Ultimate Top 10 Lists*, June 10, 2008, http://listverse.com/2008/06/10/top-15-amazing-facts-about-the-human-body.

5. "Amazing Facts About Our Body," Sortlifeout.co.uk, accessed October 20, 2010, http://sortlifeout.co.uk/body.htm.

Jean Blackmer is the publishing manager for MOPS International, author of *Boy-sterous Living! Celebrating Your Loud and Rowdy Life with Sons*, coauthor of *Where Women Walked: Powerful True Stories of Women's Perseverance and God's Provision*, and a regular contributor to MOPS publications. She has also written numerous articles for publications including *Guideposts*, *Today's Christian Woman*, Chicken Soup for the Soul books, and others. She has an MA in journalism from the University of Colorado at Boulder. Jean and her husband, Zane, live in Boulder, Colorado, with their three sons.

What Mom Doesn't Need a Break?

This collection of short devotionals meets moms where they are, helping them find a little peace and quiet in the midst of their crazy days.

Available Wherever Books Are Sold